Stop stealing
my words!.

(you lovely Mum.)

Lots of love
Oliver.

May 2016

Inspiring Sustainable Behaviour

What's the answer to inspiring sustainable behaviour? It starts with a question – or nineteen. With this simple and inspiring guide you'll learn how to ask for persistent, pervasive, and near-costless change by uncovering our hidden quirks, judgmental biases, and apparent irrationalities.

The only change you'll need to make is how you ask.

Business and government are under pressure to account for their carbon output and reduce resource-stress irrespective of the products they sell, the services they perform, or the policy and legislation they enact. Set against this is the congregation of popular culture and popular science around a desire to understand how we behave (the rise in popularity of behavioural economics is a testament to this). However, business and government are forging ahead without their marketing and communications departments because they're unable to help communicate or design initiatives effectively.

The '19 different ways to ask for change' offer a solution to this perfect storm by wrangling environmental psychology, behavioural economics, decision theory, and a good dose of common sense together in a potent handbook for marketers and legislators to ask for and sell sustainable behaviour by using the right words, and the right images, at the right time. It explains how simplification isn't always the solution, an action can be the most successful question, and a default answer can do wonders. It explores why short-term memory tasks change our behaviour, how 'singing roads' regulate speed, and that commitment gaps change outcomes; how our worry-profile is the same as an Argentinean farmer's, why knowledge of what kills you is irrelevant but asking about behaviour that kills is deadly, and what a chimpanzee's tea-party tells us about the effect of ownership on decision-making. There's the Lisbon stairs, a Chinese minister, and Kaiser Wilhelm II who makes us late for appointments twice a year.

This timely book will be of great value to scholars and practitioners whose work relates to reducing carbon emissions and resource-stress with a particular emphasis on communications. It offers practical solutions and easily understandable concepts for policymakers and professionals in marketing and communications departments, using research from a range of cognitive-behavioural theories.

Oliver Payne began his career in digital marketing at the dawn of the internet era. He went on to spend over a decade at Saatchi & Saatchi and Ogilvy creating innovative communications for some of the world's biggest companies. Frustrated with established marketing practices, especially around sustainability, he decided to set up his own agency – The Hunting Dynasty – to create powerful behavioural communications that use our hidden quirks and apparent irrationalities to create lasting change.

Inspiring Sustainable Behaviour

19 ways to ask for change

Oliver Payne

Routledge
Taylor & Francis Group

LONDON AND NEW YORK

First published 2012
by Routledge
2 Park Square, Milton Park, Abingdon, Oxon OX14 4RN

Simultaneously published in the USA and Canada
by Routledge
711 Third Avenue, New York, NY 10017

Routledge is an imprint of the Taylor & Francis Group, an informa business

British Library Cataloguing in Publication Data
A catalogue record for this book is available from the British Library

Library of Congress Cataloging-in-Publication Data
Payne, Oliver G.
Inspiring sustainable behaviour : 19 ways to ask for change / Oliver G. Payne.
p. cm.
1. Economics--Psychological aspects. 2. Economics--Environmental aspects. 3. Consumer behavior. 4. Environmentalism--Psychological aspects. 5. Environmental policy--Psychological aspects. 6. Environmental psychology. I. Title.
HB74.P8P29 2012
338.9'27--dc23
2011042483

ISBN: 978-1-84971-400-6 (hbk)
ISBN: 978-0-203-12163-4 (ebk)

Typeset in Sabon
by Saxon Graphics Ltd, Derby

Printed and bound in Great Britain by
CPI Antony Rowe, Chippenham, Wiltshire

To our hidden quirks, judgmental biases,
and apparent irrationalities

Contents

Acknowledgments

You can only write a book one word at a time, on one keyboard, with one pair of hands. It can be rather solitary. However, deciding what to write – and perhaps more importantly deciding what not to write – is the sum of many influences, from many people. I'd like to thank them all.

I've had the pleasure of being near some huge brains whose clarity and insight helped tremendously – Colwyn Elder was great to bounce ideas around with, I had the pleasure to spend years working with Rory Sutherland, and Nick Southgate's insight into advertising and cognitive-behavioural theories was always invaluable. I spent many years working day-in day-out with great writers from whom I learned all of my good habits from, and none of the bad: David Shearer, Max Vinall, Ruth Adair, Ed Cox, Pavlos Themistocleous, and Bo Hellberg. A special thanks to Ed, who gave good advice and tight editing on important parts of the manuscript, and thanks to Alister Nimmo and Helen Brocklebank who read and made helpful comments, too.

All the people who asked me to speak either formally or informally helped me strengthen parts of the book: Shane Snow when he was at the UK's Department for Transport, Warren Hatter from Ripple, Sol Slade and Celia Cole at The Forum for the Future, Dr Victoria Hands at the London School of Economics and Political Science, and Sylvia Rowley at both the Green Alliance Think Tank and the *Guardian*.

Many thanks go to Sarah, Franc, Annie, and Spock who made sure I had to leave my desk everyday during the research phase, and to Geoffrey and Waveney Payne who made sure I had a bolt-hole while I was writing – all of whom kept me sane. Thanks to Charlotte Russell and Khanam Virjee at Taylor & Francis/Routlege (Earthscan) for sweeping me effortlessly and professionally to the end of the project. Thanks to Frances Brown who made me appear polished. And thanks to Dr Nick Bellorini and Gudrun Freese who looked after me at the beginning, and a special thanks to Nick who originally signed me.

Without these people this would have been a very different book. Or, perhaps, no book at all. Thank you.

Oliver Payne, October 2011

Preface

'If you said, I want to create a problem that people don't care about, you would probably come up with global warming', says Dan Ariely, a behavioural economist from Duke University.[1] And he's right, partly because its effects are distant in four dimensions: 'not here', 'not now', 'not me', and 'not clear'.

Today's solutions mostly involve side- or downshifting. And 'selling' that is tricky because it's rarely considered desirable – yet the creation of desire is where the communication businesses do their best work.

Ideally we'd present the world to ourselves in a way that encourages our choices to fall in favour of reducing resource-stress without force or penalty. But that's a tough ask.

However, I found a route to the answer. And it's horribly simple: 'despite being generally capable and smart, we are highly context dependent'.[2]

'How' we communicate alters our response more than 'what' we communicate. It is indiscriminate. It happens in the corridors of the political elite, as much as on the signs at the local refuse centre. It happens in the boardrooms as much as in the post-rooms of businesses large and small. It happens when you sign for a house, and it happens when you write a quick note on the fridge door. Context is everything, and you can't remove it – there is no neutral, odourless, colourless way of communicating. It is persistent and pervasive, and its effects are immediate. Also, it is near costless to enact.

A persistent, pervasive, immediate, and inexpensive communication approach is a pretty powerful thing to have.

Whilst it may be relatively easy to describe, efforts and experiments to explain how it works are ongoing. Many of these experiments are hidden in jargon-laden academic journals; some are expressed and explained in more popular outlets. But however the information is delivered, researchers and academics are constantly exploring new ways of understanding how we engage with the world around us.

In order to make sense of this valuable knowledge specifically in service of inspiring sustainable behaviour, I inhabit a strange space: I'm pulling together marketing on one arm, psychology and environmental psychology on another; I'm pulling cognitive-behavioural theories – behavoural economics and behavioural decision theory – with one leg, and legislature and product design on the other. In the space they meet, this book exists.

As is inevitable in scribing an area of exploration, there are edges. And it's often at the edges you find the most interesting effects – despite the fact that technology and infrastructure design are not normally something the marketing and legislative communities are involved with, a marketer or legislator primed with the lessons of cognitive-behavioural research can legitimately discuss ways to *help develop products to be marketed*, rather than simply *marketing products that have been developed*.

So not only has a mix of marketing psychology, environmental psychology, behavioural decision theory, and behavioural economics unlocked a way of presenting choice in favour of sustainability around our existing infrastructure in a way that's effective immediately, is serviceable far in the future, works overtly and covertly, is near costless to enact, and doesn't need propping up to act persistently – it also helps create new innovations and developments that could see us solve our resource-stress for generations to come.

This is a long way from trying to sell side- or downshifting.

And in a way, it is so far removed that this book is about sustainability only in so much as that's the prism through which I've shot the methods.

So how do you get it to work? How do you move from theory to practice – where does the rubber hit the road?

It's simple: All you have to do is *ask*.

Notes

1 Colorado State University (22 December 2009), *Extension Clean Energy Outreach*, Leigh Fortson, online, www.ext.colostate.edu/energy/091222.html (accessed October 2011).

2 J. Fuller, 'Heads you die: bad decisions, choice architecture, and how to mitigate predictable irrationality', Per Capita Research Group, July 2009.

Introduction

'Eat, drink, and be merry, for tomorrow we die.'

English proverb

1.

Vittorio was under attack. Ethiopian tribesmen had pushed him back up the hill of Daga Roba, near Galla in Ethiopia. They asked him to put down his weapons. He refused. As an Italian army officer and gentlemen explorer he'd got into (and out of) many sticky situations. But on this Wednesday, in March 1897, there was one vital difference: whilst he'd been mapping the Omo River, Ethiopia had declared war on Italy.[1]

Vittorio looked the classic Italian army officer: mustachioed, smartly dressed, and stiff of resolve. As a young man he'd transferred to Eritrea with dreams of heroism, and set about exploring the region. For his first expedition he took one hundred men to map the source of the Giuba. He met with mixed success: thirty-five were killed, including two while hunting hippopotamus. He returned to Italy to plan his next exploration and spotted an opportunity on the border of Ethiopia and Kenya – if he could follow and map the Omo river to its conclusion, maybe that would secure his place in history.

Little did he know.

The Daga Roba skirmish with the Ethiopian tribesmen was serious. Both sides had rifles. The tailored uniforms of the Italians stood them apart from the lose-fitting long shirts of their enemy. The Ethiopians, emboldened by a recent victory over the Italian army at Adowa, were on home ground. And with shields and swords as well as rifles, they were as effective at close range as they were from a distance.

In that skirmish, on a Wednesday in March 1897, Vittorio was killed.

He was thirty-six years, seven months, and six days old. His final resting place lay unmarked and unknown. A cruel irony for a man who'd spent his life mapping the region. However, his work was not in vain. He'd mapped a part of the planet so significant it would re-define the foundations of our existence.

In 1967, a team of archaeologists found the remains of a 195,000-year-old *Homo sapiens* woman on the banks of the Omo river - Vittorio's Omo river.[2]

She is the earliest anatomically modern human ever found:[3] a relative of the single tribe of around two hundred people who left the African continent thousands of years later and to whom the entire human race outside of Africa owes its existence.

2.

195,000 years ago the Omo valley was a flat, dry grassland. The Omo snaked through the valley fringed with lush green forest into Lake Turkana. Lake levels were much higher then – the river entered the lake at Kibish, about sixty miles north of today's position. Yearly floods of the Omo river delta provided a rhythm to life, and a nutrient-rich soil for the vegetation.

Modern man walked through the savanna in groups of about twenty or thirty, and made little mark on the world apart from some chipped stones used for cutting and scraping.

As time went by, these groups began to trade. It helped them survive famine and drought. Around this trade, items of symbolism and ritual developed – beads, ochre, and bone. [4]

When glaciation lowered the world's sea levels by about eighty metres some 65,000 years ago, the Red Sea shrank and two hundred modern humans moved north. [5]

A move that would change the face of the planet. [6]

Life was tough, so working together was vital. Language developed. We are not so far removed from those days. Only as recently as 2005, the last speaker of a language called Bo died[7] – it was one of the Great Andamanese languages dating back to a time when that small group of a few hundred *Homo sapiens* ventured out of Africa.

The development of language is thought to be associated with symbolic thought and cultural creativity, and expression of this in both art and burial denotes knowledge, awareness, and intention. Indeed, it is the earliest evidence of behavioural modernity.[8]

Whether behavioural modernity was a result of a dramatic biological brain upgrade, a steady transition, or trading networks dense enough to cross-pollinate ideas, the effects were striking: Social, technological, and local knowledge could be apportioned among the group rather than reside Xerox-like in each individual.[9] Something as simple as the ability to warn fellow tribesmen of a dangerous animal's location, for example, meant that those who took the advice survived, and those who ignored it were killed. We are descendants of the survivors – the ones that feared loss.

Eventually, our ability for structured thinking and ethical judgment (despite some blind-spots) would stand us apart from other species.

As man made more tools and weapons, and became more adept at communication and organization, he was able both to mechanize and to refine his hunting technique. Spreading across southern Asia, Europe, Russia, and the Americas across the Bering Strait, he left a trail of increasingly sophisticated ritual, language, and society.[10]

3.

In 1907, a statue of Vittorio was erected outside the train station in his hometown of Parma, Italy. His boyhood self would have looked up at this towering statue with wide-eyed amazement.

Vittorio's statue has significance beyond his success as an explorer. It was erected at a time when industrialization was transforming our world, and at a place that led the charge – the railway.

Never before had such a large volume of material been carried so quickly, over such long distances. The advent of the daily national newspaper owes its existence to the railway.[11] Moving atoms of paper and ink over larger distances every day was simply not possible by horse or river barge. The railways also created standardized time. In England the sun sets a few minutes apart in London and Bristol. Local time was synchronized accordingly, but this played havoc with the train timetables. In 1880 standardization was imposed.[12]

Industrialization was delivering a standard of housing, food, sanitation, and education previously unknown. Life expectancy rocketed. Until about 1800, the average hovered around the twenty- to thirty-year mark and had done so for thousands of years.[13] From 1850 onwards, life expectancy in England increased by six hours per day on average.[14] So a child born a week after another would have a life expectancy nearly two days longer. Today, children born after the millennium are more likely than not to live to be one hundred years old.[15]

Thousands of years of short and brutal lives have taught us that *a bird in the hand is worth two in the bush*. Is this still the case?

Wealth has increased ninefold since the beginning of industrialization.[16] In the 1800s, one hour of light cost six hours of work. Today, you only need perform one second of work to purchase an hour of light. Even in 1950 you needed only a handful of work-seconds to buy the same.[17] And that's not because industrialization has increased the production of candles. It's found newer and orders-of-magnitude denser forms of energy.

In two hundred or so short years we've gone from steam and iron, to coal and steel, to oil, plastics, and mass electrification.

This has allowed the production of goods and services unimaginable even a century ago, let alone 40,000 years ago: a choice of calories, doctored edible produce and extracted vitamins tailored to the exact needs of the human body. We've developed non-tangible things like law, privacy, and rights. And money. And we can communicate instantaneously, anywhere in the world – we create more information every forty-eight hours than was created between the dawn of civilization and 2003.[18] There have only been about 20,000 generations over the last half a million years – and less than 10,000 since our direct ancestors wandered the Omo valley. And yet in the last four generations we've transformed from a local animal to a global one that can circumnavigate the world in a day.

Evolutionarily speaking, this is a baffling world.

We understand our physical limitations much better than our cognitive ones – perhaps because our emotional judgments are better tested than our intellectual assessments: we jump a mile at snakes, but rarely fear electric cable; We get spooked in the dark, but cross the road without looking.[19] We are still imprinted with the mores of a short, brutal, provincial life.

Delaying gratification traditionally has such a high cost it is still woven into our language: *a bird in the hand is worth two in the bush; eat, drink, and be merry, for tomorrow we die.* We fear loss much more than the pleasure of gain[20] because this strategy has always survived over profligacy and delay.

With our instincts defined by a few hundred *Homo sapiens* and refined over nearly 150,000 years, the last century or so of incredibly rapid change hasn't even begun to affect our behaviour. We are ancient creatures living in modern times.

We are fit for a world that no longer surrounds us.

Part I

The expected

All the questions you'd expect to ask, but not in the way you'd expect to ask them

As the saying goes, even the worst piece of communication only needs two things changed: all the words, and all the images. As trite as that sounds, there is some truth in it.

We'll explore how words like *tax, offset, climate change,* and *global warming* can evoke responses in ways you wouldn't expect, and how imagery – either synthetic or constructed – affects our decisions in covert ways. Are these principles at the root of variously attributed lament: 'Half of all advertising works, I just wish I knew which half'?

We'll look at how a tiny hammer in a box that could kill a cat is on a par with asking a question. How the strength of your desire is nothing to do with what you say and everything to do with the fact that you said it – and that can kill you. And why your highfalutin 'flights of fancy' are triggered by the 'why': Lévi-Strauss is involved.

Later in this section issues of timing and incentive keep us on familiar ground, but are expressed in unfamiliar ways. (You'll want to keep the snack food out of reach if you're on a health kick when you read about bunched messaging and cognitive load; the reasons will become clear.) Incentives and incentivising behaviour focus on cash and fun. Cash is an obvious and lazy place to go (the BOGOF is as much a bane of the marketer's life as is taxation for a legislator), but cash incentives for resource-reducing behaviour can be inexpensive if the correct question is asked: it's a cheap thrill.

As expected, welcome to the Expected.

1   Just ask

'If you want anything just ask for it, old sport.'

F. Scott Fitzgerald, *The Great Gatsby* (1925)

In 1935, in an attempt to illustrate the bizarreness of quantum mechanics, Erwin Schrödinger devised a thought experiment to show that the act of observation can change the observed. He imagined a cat sealed in a box with a phial of poison, a radioactive particle, a Geiger counter, and a tiny hammer. The radioactive particle roamed the box. If it was detected by the Geiger counter the tiny hammer would break the phial of poison, which would kill the cat.

That's not the bizarre bit.

Shortly after the experiment had begun, the cat would exist as both potentially alive and potentially dead: that's the bizarre bit. This simultaneous state would resolve only when the lid was opened and the cat observed. It's only this act of observation that resolves the state of the cat.[1]

The lesson Schrödinger sought to highlight is there's no way to engage with the world without affecting it.

He's right.

Schrödinger's car

It was long thought that strength of desire was a good measure of the likelihood of action – and to find the strength of desire, you just ask. Say Fishbein and Ajzen: 'If one wants to know whether or not an individual will perform a given behaviour, the simplest and probably most efficient thing one can do is to ask the individual whether he [or she] intends to perform that behaviour.'[2]

Vicki Morwitz from the Stern School, New York, and Gavan Fitzsimons of the Wharton School, Pennsylvania, discovered something quite different when they asked 40,000 people about the strength of their desire to purchase a new car: *Simply asking about the strength of desire disproportionately increased action.*[3]

That wasn't supposed to happen.

The actual rates of car purchase among the group in the following six months shot up to over 35% above average.

Simply by measuring the state, they changed it.

This effect's been dubbed the Mere Measurement effect (even though there's nothing mere about its effect). It tells us that our response to an initial-intent question changes our subsequent evaluations by activating an existing attitude – and that attitude remains accessible and pronounced for some time. However, if there were no existing inclination one would not appear. Much like a countryside path – if you have a groove, you'll get a rut. So of those 40,000 with existing inclination to purchase, their attitude was amplified. This amplification of intent is not solely about purchase: Greenwald, Carnot, Beach, and Young saw the probability of voting increase by 25% for people who had been asked about their voting intention for the following day.[4]

These are big numbers.

And they have been observed elsewhere, affecting computer purchases, volunteering, exercising, and recycling – and even affecting harmful behaviours like food choice[5] and drug taking.[6] It may even be responsible for killing people: well-meaning government and charity drug support programmes often question heavy and serious drug addicts about their previous patterns of drug use in order to allocate future resources efficiently, thereby invoking the Mere Measurement effect and so increasing their drug-use rates.

The workings from this data are contested.[7] However, in a similar study of New Jersey teenagers on a suicide prevention programme, those that were told about the worryingly large number of teens who take their own lives became more likely to see suicide as an answer to their own problems.[8] Similarly, an eating disorder help-group for young women involved many women describing their harmful eating. Participants had more disorder symptoms after attending the groups.[9] (See also chapter 12, 'Ask using the right authority'.)

Death and disorder are extreme examples, but the problematic effect of the Mere Measurement effect doesn't end there – it questions the foundations of market research: 'The American Marketing Association (AMA) code of ethics clearly segregates the conduct of marketing research from any form of sales or opinion-influencing activity.'[10] I think we can safely say that 'opinion-influencing activity' is the definition of the Mere Measurement effect.

Oops.

And it gets even more fascinating. After 40,000 people were exposed to the survey question in the Fitzsimons and Morwitz study, it became apparent that car owners increase their likelihood of purchasing from their current manufacturer, while those who don't own a car increase their likelihood of purchasing from any one of the frequently advertised brands.[11]

Frequently. Advertised. Brands.

By definition, a manufacturer of an electric car has a product that's both new to the market and a *new category* for many consumers. They'd do great business simply by advertising. It's almost irrelevant *what* they say, only that the brand is exposed. Or maybe they should do a simple survey?

The Mere Measurement effect was evoked from a 'simple' question that puts the receiver as the main actor in a scenario. Imaging other people in scenarios is not as effective in changing subsequent actions – this is why 'your new car' is so powerful. But what happens if we ask a more nuanced or complex question?

Nuanced questions change outcomes too (as if you hadn't guessed), but it depends on how the question is structured: imagining positive, negative, and avoidance outcomes affects outcomes differently. [12] Understanding this is vital from a sustainable point of view.

A positive statement more readily accesses an existing attitude than a negative statement, so your 'mere' question will get more of a response.[13] 'Positive' usually translates as aspirational – like ownership of a new car ('Are you going to buy a new car?'). But positive aspiration is a little tricky to elicit for products or services that require an obvious side- or down-shift – the products and services that are seen as negative.

A positive or neutral statement seems to work best when asked 'with the grain' to keep mental calculations and translations uncomplicated. For instance, don't ask *how many times do you put the bins out per month?* if the 'with the grain' answer is once every fortnight. Don't ask *how many times per month do you have a haircut?* when the 'with the grain' question is *how many weeks do you wait before you next visit?* In short, don't put any unnecessary calculations in there.[14]

A negative statement, like *can you see yourself not eating sugary foods?*, seems to have two characteristics: our 'imagined state' is poorly constructed because it requires a greater load on working memory than imagining positive or alternative scenes; that which we manage to construct in our 'imagined state' frequently goes AWOL. Information about 'not doing' something seems to be treated as casually as a trivial Post-It note.[15] Behaviour is rarely changed. This is a perennial problem for the Sustainaratti. Indeed it is a perennial problem for the overall challenge of mitigating the effects of climate change: the upstream cost versus the downstream benefit often requires the evocation of a negative feeling now for the promise of a positive one in the future (and of course that benefit is for someone else, in some other place, at some point in the future, in an unclear way, which makes it a whole heap of awkward – see chapter 7, 'Ask for a commitment (in the future)').

An 'avoidance' construction can help in this case: 'What is the likelihood you'll avoid X?' It seems much easier for us to imagine ourselves performing the necessary actions to avoid something rather than the negative construct of *not* doing something.

But, however constructed, we tend to want the shortest route, so we ignore the negative 'imagined state' and grab for positive, or, failing that, avoidance. In this sense our imagination is like a river trying to find the shortest path to lower ground, where the shortest path is a positive construct. The only exception is if the 'shortest path' is a negative statement that chimes with an existing negative attitude (a socially undesirable behaviour – like murder), because it acts much like a positive statement in the sense that 'not doing it' is good in a socially acceptable way.[16] A pseudo-positive, perhaps?

Both avoidance and positive questions are more palatable and memorable. They do more than prime behaviour – they create an implementation imprint that endures after the question that affects our evaluation and subsequent behaviour.[17]

––––––––––––––

'Simply asking' is one of the most inexpensive ways of communicating. There really isn't a great deal of infrastructure involved – only clipboards or web pages. But by being both persistent and near costless to enact, it seems the Mere Measurement effect is anything but 'mere'.

You weren't aware? All you had to do was ask.

A slice of life

Marlene Schwartz is the Deputy Director of the Rudd Center for Food Policy and Obesity at Yale University. She took on a problem that the United States' National School Lunch Program (*sic*) had been trying to solve since 1947: to ensure that American schoolchildren have access to a nutritionally balanced and affordable lunch.[18]

For 60 years they've been trying. And failed.

American schoolchildren were malnourished in 1947 because of a lack of calories. In 2007 – sixty years later – American schoolchildren were still malnourished despite having access to vast quantities of calories. Why? Because the consumption of nourishing foods like fruits and vegetables was considerably lower than needed. A school district's Health Advisory Committee had a hunch how they could increase the nutritional intake of pupils.

They thought they could solve this problem simply by asking a question.

They drafted in Marlene Schwartz to run the test. Two schools were selected, both with the same fruit and fruit juice options on the school dinner menu. She asked one school to have the dinner ladies say nothing, and the other school have the dinner ladies ask every pupil 'Would you like fruit or fruit juice with your lunch?' A simple, innocuous question to the uninitiated. Without the question, 60% of pupils took a serving. With the question, 90% of schoolchildren took a serving of fruit or fruit juice.

Success?

The experiment could've ended there. But the behaviour they wanted to test was the amount of fruit *eaten*, not the amount of fruit *chosen*. Here's the interesting bit: *once the fruit was on the tray it was eaten in the same proportion in both schools.*

That means that nearly 70% of pupils *ate* fruit at lunch when asked 'Would you like fruit or fruit juice?' compared to fewer that 40% of the pupils in the no-question school.

Juicy data.

2   Ask using the right words

'A word in earnest is as good as a speech.'
Charles Dickens, *Bleak House* (1852–3)

Advertising agencies make a lot of advertisements for well-known brands, businesses, and governments. And sometimes they make them for businesses and initiatives we know little about. (Although if that condition remains, they've not done very well.) Rarely do they make them about themselves. If they do, only marketing directors see them: there are no big budgets, and no big media spends. As a consequence, many are more phosphorus than campfire – burning quickly and brightly rather than providing a more sustained warmth and welcome.

But a few do have longevity.

In the early 1990s, employee number 16 of a sleepy Miami advertising agency wrote a self-promotional ad that still seduces twenty years later because it gets at the heart of asking a question using the right words. It was made as a press advert. It showed two images side-by-side. In one image was a man hitchhiking by the side of a road holding a cardboard sign at waist height, and written on it in black pen was the name of a US city. It could've been any place, and it could've been any hitchhiker, on any road, on any day. Above it was one bold-type word: 'Sales'. The other image was similar: a man hitchhiking by the side of a road holding a cardboard sign at waist height. Written on his sign in black pen was the line 'Mom's for Thanksgiving'. Above it was one bold-type word: 'Marketing'.

This advertisement intended to show that the difference between sales and marketing was a compelling message, to show how seductive they can be, and to show that the agency knew how to create them. It is, they are, and they knew. More precisely, the person who knew was employee number 16: Alex Bogusky. By 1991, at 31 years of age, he was the Creative Director of the agency that wrote the hitchhiker ad, and one that would go on to be nearly a thousand people strong, and win all of the world's top awards – more than once.

Knowing that different words elicit different responses is obvious to most of us (we all know 'I love you' and 'I hate you' will create different responses).

But understanding how words with subtly different meanings and contexts can create wildly different responses isn't so obvious.

That's why you need to ask with the right words.

Mandatory option

In 2008 a group of middle-aged men and women in the USA were tested on their responses to two labels that had the same meaning, but were worded differently.[1]

The group had a representative mix of political affiliations, and was split in two. The beginning of the experiment required each participant to read a sheet of paper containing an explanation of carbon reduction policies that – if implemented – would raise the price of goods and services.

For one group, part of the explanation said: 'The goal of a **carbon offset**, which may or may not be mandatory, is therefore to fund these efforts and ensure that the price of an activity reflects the true cost to society.'

For the other group, part of the explanation said: 'The goal of a **carbon tax**, which may or may not be mandatory, is therefore to fund these efforts and ensure that the price of an activity reflects the true cost to society.'

One version said 'tax', the other 'offset'[2]. This was the crux of the experiment.

After this explanation, both groups were given a sheet containing a list of everyday items like fuel, electricity providers, and computers. Each item was presented with a pair of prices: one price 'as is', and one price 'as would be' if it included the extra 'carbon tax', or 'offset' charge (depending on the group). For example, a round trip flight from New York to Los Angeles was presented as $345 base price, and $352[3] with the extra carbon charge.[4]

Fifty per cent of Democrats in the groups elected to pay more for a carbon tax after reading about its benefits, where it would be spent, and seeing the extra item cost comparison. Ten per cent of the Republicans and Independents did the same. This is not news.

What is news, however, is the fact that they were all *equally likely* to choose the more expensive product or service when it was billed as an 'offset'. Fifty per cent of the group jumped onboard: 'when participants considered the offset, there were no differences in choices between political parties, but when they considered the tax, there was a strong decreasing trend.' It is a fair representation of each political affiliation's beliefs.

It doesn't end there.

They had one more test up their sleeve. They added the word 'mandatory' to the labels: '*mandatory* carbon tax'; '*mandatory* carbon offset'.

A '*mandatory* carbon offset' plays fast and loose with the meaning of words: it is logically comparable to a '*mandatory* carbon tax' in both spirit and execution because they are both unavoidable – in practice they are both a tax. The results of the name difference are surprising.

Everyone liked '*mandatory* carbon offset'.

Democrats, Republicans, and Independents all gave it approximately a five on a seven-point scale, with seven being 'definitely' pay it. They were all responding in a way they had never done before to a mandatory payment – similarly, and positively.

This selection volte face is due to the use of language, says Tversky: 'people choose, in effect, between descriptions of options rather than between the options themselves'.[5]

Hardisty, Johnson, and Weber argue that labels – the attribute's frame – determine query order, and query order can either accentuate or attenuate embedded values. In this case, the 'mandatory offset' attenuated the natural 'mandatory tax' concerns of Republicans.

By way of a different example, someone who values fashion over functionality will naturally focus on the fashion aspects of a coat before querying its functional aspects, but if on initial inspection they are asked about the practicalities of the coat this will accentuate this aspect, effectively reducing the importance of the embedded fashion value. This changes consideration, and can change the final decision: 'manipulation of query order showed that reversing queries from their natural implicit order to an explicit unnatural order eliminated the endowment effect'.[6]

The endowment effect states that we value that which we own more highly than that which we don't (although it may be to do with the fact that we fear the loss of that which we own more than we value having it). We 'own' the values by which we navigate the world, so they are rarely shifted, and are the first place we go to inform our decision-making (unless the query order is contrary to our embedded values).

Query order effects were observed in this experiment on purpose, but you can be pretty sure they are unknowingly manipulating the consideration of decisions in the most trivial as well as the most important of decisions.

Money by any other name

Do we name things as we find them? Or do we find them as they're named? It's the latter, it seems.

In the UK, the government allocates payments to households inhabited by the elderly to supplement increased heating costs during the winter. It's called a Winter Fuel Payment, and contains a perfect contradiction: it's a direct cash transfer but it's named with a specific purpose.

Why is this a contradiction? Because standard economic theory tells us that cash is fungible – any pound sterling can be substituted for any other, so the naming of cash or cash equivalents should have no effect on spending patterns. But the Institute for Fiscal Studies found robust evidence that the labelling of payments affects how they're spent. In Households examined, for every £100 given as 'cash', £3 will be spent on fuel, but for every £100 given as 'Winter Fuel Payment', £41 will be spent on fuel.

So even if a cash transfer is unconditional (you can spend it on *anything*) their 'evidence implies that the label of this particular transfer [Winter Fuel Payment] has a critical impact on the behavioural response displayed by those who receive it'. [7]

A pound is a pound is a pound – except when it's not.

But is this a criticism only of the elderly? Criticism of those bamboozled by government and misinterpretations of the law? No. Even the financially astute fall prey to naming quirks.

In 1982, Leroy Gross wrote a book called *Manual for Stockbrokers*. He examined one of the biggest challenges for them – selling stocks and shares that have lost money. The old Wall Street maxim guides brokers to 'cut your losers short and let your winners ride', which is something a rational actor in a rational world would do. But we are not rational actors in a rational world, and we do have a problem: we hang on to losers. Gross characterized this folly as 'getevenitus'.

He gave enlightened instruction to brokers who manage money for other people to help soothe the 'getevenitus' wound: a big challenge is getting a client to close a position (because it crystallizes loss), take the money, and then re-invest in new stock. It requires an 'act of faith' and involves lots of painful loss. He advises describing it with a different formulation of words: 'The two separate transactions (moving out of the loss and moving into the new position) are made to flow together by the magic words "Transfer your assets".' [8] 'Transferring assets' is a truthful explanation, as is 'selling and re-investing', yet they create wildly different responses.

In both instances – Winter Fuel Payment and stockbrokers – the use of language is appealing to a quirk called 'mental accounting'.

It states that we give money different values depending on where we store it, with the 'store' being our construct. Money in a savings account has more spendy-friction than current cash in our pocket, and even more spendy-friction than money yet to be earned. This is the reason why people will dedicate a larger absolute contribution to their pension from pay-rises anticipated in the future than from wages earned now.

John Godek and Kyle Murray looked at how unstable fuel prices affected private drivers' mental accounting, and found that price spikes usually evoked a feeling that the overall cost of living had risen. It hadn't, but this constricted spending decisions in every part of life. They found it was being accounted for in a 'comprehensive account', rather than in a narrowly focused 'topical account'. This could be adjusted by language. They say: 'our results suggest that price changes should be framed to invoke topical (i.e. within specific consumption decisions) rather than comprehensive (i.e. overall lifestyle and spending) mental accounts'. [9]

Gary Belsky and Thomas Gilovich (financial journalist and psychology professor, respectively), authors of *Why Smart People Make Big Money Mistakes and How to Correct Them*, put mental accounting on a par with Prospect Theory – the fundamental concept of behavioural economics: 'If

Richard Thaler's concept of mental accounting is one of two pillars upon which the whole of behavioural economics rests, then prospect theory is the other.'[10]

Money, by lots of other names.

The why and wherefore

The French anthropologist Claude Lévi-Strauss notes that Western societies constructed distal concepts like geography and astrology before developing the proximal ones, like psychology.[11] Liberman, Trope, and Stephan suggest this is because theoretical reasoning is easier to apply the further away in time and space you project. If this is the case, our linguistic phrasing might reflect, and perhaps affect, our perception of the timing of events. To test this they constructed a study called 'The effect of level of construal on the temporal distance of activity enactment'.[12]

The test had four parts. The second was beautifully recursive: it looked at how we imagine the time span of actions and events that relate to *our own goals* to see if that affected what we think about *our own goals*. It did this by testing how far in the future we envision an action if we're asked 'why' we want to do it, versus being asked 'how' we're going to achieve it. The thinking being that 'why' questions create a distal interpretation and 'how' questions evoke a more proximal appreciation: or 'why' is for highfalutin 'flights of fancy' and 'how' is more practical and concrete.

To make it deeply personal, participants listed three goals in advance of the experiment. They were asked nested questions. If a goal were 'taking a vacation' they'd be asked why they'd like to go. If 'in order to rest', they'd again be asked why. If they said 'in order to renew my energy' they'd finally be asked to write why they'd like to renew their energy. The 'how' test followed the same construction and had a comparable example.

When the results came in, the average expectation of the length of time before enacting these goals was longer in the 'why' condition compared to the 'how'.

'How' is more concrete and immediate, the 'why' more cerebral and distant.

Dr Sabine Pahl, from the Department of Psychology, University of Plymouth, UK, has worked with this distal/proximal quirk in reference to perceptions of climate change and perceptions of the actions to mitigate it. In her studies she found that '"Why" triggers greater distance than "how" in perceptions of climate change.'[13] The word swap directly brings the perception of climate change effects closer by making them seem more concrete. Similarly, and perhaps more interestingly, her research showed that actions that create sustainable behaviour – from investing in renewables, to recycling, and much more besides – were predicted to be performed sooner if explained in 'how' rather than 'why' terms. (This was true for first person and third person tests, pretty much.)

This ability to make the problems of climate change appear more real and make the solutions appear more achievable can help change behaviour today and sell the technology and infrastructure for the future. As Pahl describes: 'Psychological Distance . . . seems to have great potential for sustainability-related perceptions and behaviour.'[14]

That's what we're looking for.

You say tom-ay-tow, I say tom-ah-tow

The terms 'global warming' and 'climate change' are frequently interchanged. This is both incorrect and unhelpful. From a technical point of view it's incorrect – global warming refers to an increase in temperature near ground level, and climate change refers to the effects of a warming planet – and from a linguistic point of view it's unhelpful because each term creates a frame that alters the debate across the political divide.

A study of US Think Tanks by Schuldt, Konrath, and Schwarz called "Global warming" or "climate change"? Whether the planet is warming depends on question wording[15] found that, of the two phrases, conservatives frequently used the term 'global warming', and more liberal Think Tanks frequently used the term 'climate change'. To find out how these different words represented opinions about meteorological observations they polled thousands of respondents and asked this question:

> You may have heard about the idea that the world's temperature may have been *going up* [*changing*] over the past 100 years, a phenomenon sometimes called '*global warming*' ['*climate change*'].
>
> What is your personal opinion regarding whether or not this has been happening?
>
> 1 = Definitely **has not been** happening;
> 2 = Probably **has not been** happening;
> 3 = Unsure, but leaning toward it **has not been** happening;
> 4 = Not sure eitherway;
> 5 = Unsure, but leaning toward it **has been** happening;
> 6 = Probably **has been** happening;
> 7 = Definitely **has been** happening (bold in original).The italics and bolding are theirs. The responses were presented with radio buttons allowing only a single answer to be selected.

Those on the more liberal political spectrum were unaffected by the wording (87% versus 86%), but conservatives were less likely to endorse 'global warming' (44%) than 'climate change' (60%).

Why the difference?

Separate from this study Lorraine Whitmarsh says '"Global warming" is more often believed to have human causes and tends to be associated with . . . heat-related impacts, such as temperature increase and melting icebergs and glaciers.'[16]

In light of this association, a 'human cause' seems false in the face of unexpected cold snaps, large dumps of snow, and rains and floods – none of which are 'warm' events. Wedded to this is the fact that problematic changes in temperature of between one and four degrees not only are below our threshold of discernibility, but are surrounded by the 'noise' of circadian, seasonal, and regional temperature changes.

Schuldt, Konrath, and Schwarz's research results bear this out: 'Republican respondents were more skeptical that global climate change is a real phenomenon when an otherwise identical question was worded in terms of "global warming" rather than "climate change"'[17]

The phrase 'climate change' has no embedded temperature direction, so is able to encompass extremes of weather without contradiction. Lorraine tells us that in studies 'The term "climate change" is more readily associated with natural causes and a range of impacts.'[18] It appears less pejorative in relation to humans' actions (even though it is a criticism of them), and so offers a reading of the issues that doesn't have an embedded anthropogenic critique.

But why don't liberals care which formulation of words is used? They may have a more crystallised opinion and so the anthropogenic tension inherent in warming/snow has little power. But, however opinion is derived, the interesting outtake from Schuldt, Konrath, and Schwarz's 'question wording' study is that conservatives and liberals aren't really that far apart. When the 'climate change' formulation of words is used, 60% of Republicans and over 80% of Democrats will endorse it.

'I take the upshot of the study to be that Americans are less polarized about climate change/global warming than they may appear. Disagreement under the "climate change" frame is really fairly mild', says *The Economist* magazine.[19]

The most important thing isn't what you say; it's how you say it.

Rubbish

A trick that's been long in the marketers' toolbox is to collapse the distance between an action and its outcome. And that's exactly what San Francisco Company Golden Gate Disposal is doing with the names of their refuse bins.

They now call them *landfill* bins.

And they take a consistent approach to this new classification at every point of communication: Tracy, a San Francisco resident, called Nancy at Golden Gate Disposal for a new garbage bin: 'Ma'am, I have to tell you that we now call them landfill bins'.

That's not a throwaway comment.

Charged language

Peter Curran is a presenter on British radio station BBC Radio 4. He drove and reported on a 4,500 mile trans-European journey in an electric car.

The first paragraph of this odyssey uses language that describes a world where the 'norm' is something other than his approach:

> 'he meets major European motor manufacturers, gauges political will across the continent, *attempts to drive over the alps* and becomes multi-lingual in the phrase *"Where can I plug this in please?"*'[20] (My italics.)

The phrase 'attempts to drive over the alps' frames electric vehicles as weak, which probably chimes with most people's expectations even though DC electric motors have an incredible amount of torque (even at low revs) compared to the internal combustion engine. And the phrase 'Where can I plug this in please?' presents the car as a social outcast rather than a social norm.

Is this representation of electric vehicles well considered?

The US advertising agency Crispin Porter + Bogusky decided to do something similar. They got two employees of the Brammo electric motorbike company to ride from Detroit to Washington to retrace the journey that GM and Ford bosses took when they flew to Washington by private jet to ask for billions of dollars to bailout their ailing companies.

It is billed as a 'journey to present our president [Barack Obama] with the most energy efficient electric vehicle in America'. They continue:

> present President Obama with a *homegrown solution to the transportation crisis*. And instead of flying in a corporate jet, we're riding Brammo Enertia powercycles. We're *just a couple of guys who work for Brammo*, but we want to show that there's a *better way to get from Point A to Point B*. And we want to have a little *fun while we're doing it*.[21] (My italics.)

The phrase 'homegrown solution to the transportation crisis' paints a positive solution and a behaviour we can all aspire to. And the phrases 'Just a couple of guys who work for Brammo', 'better way to get from Point A to Point B', and 'fun while we're doing it' pitch the whole enterprise as embedded in the normal for every blue-collar US worker.

The polar opposite of the BBC's language.

Language can help define the 'norm'. Whatever the 'norm' is, it's important because it's a powerful driver of our behaviour: no one wants to be the odd-ball in the group.

3 Ask using the right images

'It's not what you look at that matters, it's what you see.'

Henry David Thoreau, 1817–62

William A. Marsteller graduated as a journalist in 1937. After various newspaper and marketing jobs, he became the advertising manager of the Rockwell Manufacturing Company. While there, he realized the importance and possibilities of market research. He thought it had a future. So much of a future, in fact, he went to see a small Chicago advertising agency called Gebhardt & Brockson. He liked it. He bought it. And a short while later, he bought the Pittsburgh office of McCarty Co. too. He merged them into a new business-to-business advertising agency called Marsteller, Gebhardt & Reed.

He was now an ad man.

By 1960 – after more mergers and deals – he had moved the headquarters to midtown New York, and a few years later he renamed the agency Marsteller Inc. His name was above the door.

His move to New York coincided with revolution inside and outside of adland. All across America the Vietnam war and the protests against it, the Summer of Love and the contraceptive pill, and liberal and adventurous music, were changing culture forever. Inside advertising agencies a 'creative revolution' was changing the business too: account managers no longer managed the client as well as writing the words of an advertisement – that role was given to a dedicated copywriter. He, or she, was paired up with a dedicated visual person (an art director) and together they would create the great television, magazine, and poster advertisements of the 1960s and the 1970s.

However, none of this had any effect on Marsteller Inc.

The cultural changes that characterized the decade, and the reorganisation of the advertising industry, were not happening at Marsteller Inc.: it was an agency more akin to its 1950s origins. It was an anomaly among its peers.[1] And yet, despite this anomaly, in 1971 it created one of the best Public Service Announcement television commercials of the twentieth century.

It's called 'The Crying Indian', and it was commissioned by the Keep America Beautiful campaign. It stars Chief Iron Eyes Cody, and first played on Earth Day in 1971:

> Chief Iron Eyes Cody paddles a Native American style canoe in a rural river. He passes some floating litter.
>
> We see industry surround the river. There are large bank-side cranes and stack pipes. Cody paddles to a sloping shale shore, steps out of his canoe, and pulls it away from the waterline. There's litter at his feet.
>
> He climbs up onto a paved roadway that runs along the side of the river. It is noisy from the hum of passing cars, and is littered. A passenger in a passing car throws a bag of rubbish out of the open window. It lands at Cody's feet.
>
> He turns to camera with his face filling the screen and a tear running down his cheek. The voice over says 'People start pollution, people can stop it.'

This campaign has won advertising awards, and is recognized by the print publication *Advertising Age* as one of the top 100 US advertising campaigns of the twentieth century.[2]

But I'm not so sure it is: while it might be asking with the right sentiment, it's not asking with the right images.

Stack pipes and car parks

In 1990 three US psychologists, Robert Cialdini, Raymond Reno, and Carl A. Kallgren researched littering behaviour.[3] They dressed a Texas car park with litterbins, and placed handbills under the windscreen wipers of parked cars. Returning car owners saw a handbill on their windscreen. They had a decision to make: keep it, place it in the litterbin, or drop it on the floor.

But it wasn't quite as simple as that.

Cialdini, Reno, and Kallgren's team switched the car park between one of two states – strewn with litter or completely clean. Did this affect behaviour? It did. The littered car park had the highest incidence of handbills discarded on the floor at just over 30%, and the clean car park had the lowest at just under 15%. This tallied with expectations – that evidence of a 'social norm' informs individual decisions. In the clean condition it is obvious that *no one else thinks littering is ok*, so you should think that too. In the littered condition it is obvious that *everyone else thinks littering is ok*, so you should think that too. Whether you act on that thought is another thing, but having those terms of reference set up is the point.

Good. Experiment done? No. Not quite.

As well as having evidence of either littering or cleanliness, how about putting a real person in the scene? This may make the social norm more salient. The team engaged an actor – a stooge – briefed to wait until an unsuspecting car owner returned, and then either walk by within eyesight doing nothing, or walk by within eyesight dropping litter.

The stooge's actions had an extraordinarily polarizing effect:

- Nearly 55% of people dropped trash when they saw the stooge drop trash in a *littered* car park.
- Only 6% of people dropped trash when they saw the stooge drop trash in a *clean* car park.

Seeing someone litter in a clean environment amplified littering as an outsider's activity – it is not prevalent, it is not approved. Seeing someone litter in a littered environment amplified littering as an insider's activity – it is prevalent, it is approved.

This 'double shot' of descriptive and injunctive norms created a difference in littering of nearly ten times. So how does that inform our opinion of Chief Iron Eyes Cody and his Crying Indian?

It seems like it'd be a bad idea to make an anti-littering television commercial that showed people littering in a littered environment, as that is likely to create the highest inclination to litter. And yet, that's exactly what Marsteller Inc. did with Chief Iron Eyes Cody. Cialdini – part of the Texas car park team – made this connection, and makes this comment: 'Public service communicators should avoid the tendency to send the normatively muddled message that a targeted activity is socially disapproved but widespread.'[4]

How are these messages having effect?

Overt information – 'please don't litter' – is routed though our cognitive capacity, and lined up against our understanding of society and its rules. We want to know what other people will approve of before we embed it as a behaviour. It is a rule-governed, calculating, reasoned effort. So while overt information *can* influence intentions, it has to negotiate a cognitive assault course first.

It seems viewing the *raw* behaviour of others plugs that 'norm' straight into our brain without having to negotiate the cognitive assault course. It is an intuitive, rapid, and associative effort. In this regard, we are quite different from the (rest of the) animal kingdom. Most animals have no cognitive assault course: normative behaviour is plugged straight in. Just as fish school, and insects swarm, the intuitive, rapid, and associative effort rules.[5]

If you do manage to engage fully with both messages – the overt wish not to litter, but the covert message that everybody does – it gets a little more tricky, because you are cast into cognitive dissonance: your 'gut' says one thing and your 'head' says another. How do we deal with dissonance?

We ignore it. Ouch.

But the Crying Indian advert was produced in the early 1970s by an agency that was a throwback to the 1950s. By now the marketers have learned the lessons, right? Wrong.

For years the UK government ran an authoritative information service called 'Act On CO2' about climate change and how communities, government, and business can reduce its effects. It was a worthy aim. Sometimes Act On CO2 commissioned television advertisements. They chose an agency unlike Marsteller Inc.: it was thrusting, dynamic, famous, modern, and global.

One advert, called 'Reflections',[6] asks the general public to drive fewer miles per week. In the absence of technological or infrastructural change, it is an immediate way of reducing carbon dioxide output because fossil fuel transport is disproportionately represented in time used/carbon output ratios. (To give some context, a typical car engine uses 1,000 times as much energy as an old filament light-bulb,[7] and a gallon of petrol represents about 15,000 times more CO_2 than a disposable plastic carrier bag.[8] It's a strategically robust decision.

The execution, however, uses almost exclusively imagery of other people in nose-to-tail traffic, aeroplanes, and traffic-filled roads while the voiceover implores you to drive less. Contradiction much? It is an almost exact copy of the Crying Indian littering advert's 'normatively muddled message'. They fell into the same trap.

The 30-second 'Reflections' television advert plays thus:

> A lorry and a van are in a traffic jam. An aeroplane is in flight above them.
>
> The voiceover tells us that CO_2 emissions from these types of vehicles contribute to climate change, with the most coming from cars.
>
> As the camera pulls back, we realize the image is reflected in the door of a car, which is parked outside a house.
>
> The visuals show a car parking in a street, and the voiceover tells us that together we can begin to make a difference by driving 5 miles less a week.

While it is a perfect example of the 'we all do this, but don't you do this' dissonance rendered in 30 seconds, one can see how they get to this visualisation: it's difficult to present a downshift like driving fewer miles as aspirational for the individual, so traffic jams and their associated *inconvenience* is a great 'reason to believe' why driving fewer miles would be beneficial to the individual. (It's probably better tackled in a medium other than television.)

But, as true as the 'reason to believe' is, it is an overt message that needs to be parsed by our cognitive apparatus at the same time as the imagery of abundant car use is pumped straight in as the 'norm'. As a contest it is a little one-sided. In a test of recycling adverts on an Arizona regional public service channel and further laboratory investigation into the descriptive and injunctive norms contained therein the team say: 'Information about social approval or disapproval affected . . . assessments of the ads' persuasiveness. Information about relative prevalence, in contrast, influenced intentions directly.'[9]

Prevalence is what really drives behaviour.

You have to see it to believe it

In 1968, David Ogilvy was appointed as Chair of the United Negro College Fund. As an advertising agency founder and copywriter, he thought he could put his skills to work in raising money for the college fund. He could. He wrote an open letter.

On Monday, 24 June it was printed and placed on the seats of every train leaving Grand Central Station in New York. It was beautifully written, as you would expect – weaving cogent argument with emotional narrative. But the trick was the backdrop. The trick was the way Ogilvy slammed the image of those he was writing about into the eyes of his readers. And it started with the first sentence: 'When this train emerges from the tunnel at 108th street this evening, look out of the window.' (The underlining is his.)[10]

He follows this by telling the reader they may even see some of the 1,125 boys and girls covered by the college fund in those New York ghettos. He continues for two pages, but by the first sentence he'd brought the invisible 'them' to life. It's difficult to do sometimes, but being able to visualise the intangible is powerful technique. So powerful, in fact, that in just one night that letter raised $26,000.

Is this technique valuable elsewhere?

Julie Goodhew, Sabine Pahl, and Tim Auburnof the Psychology and Sustainability Group at the University of Plymouth, UK have some preliminary data on the effects of visualizing heat loss.[11] They approached customers of a home decoration and DIY store who had never previously purchased any 'green' products. About 100 agreed to be involved in the year-and-a-half-long study.

Each household began with advice about the source of carbon dioxide emissions, an energy audit, information about food and waste disposal, and ways of dealing with them all. They were given £500 each to spend as they wished, to improve their efficiency.

Just over half of the households were revisited and given an additional piece of information – a thermal imaging report.

A thermal camera was trained on their homes at night and shots were taken to 'make concrete' the sources of heat loss, which was sucking the efficiency out of their energy use. Many were surprised. But the real results came when the study visited them for a third time to see if there was any lasting change. It had an astounding effect: 'If the householder saw the [thermal camera] image they were 8x more likely to have installed draught proofing than if they had not seen the image.'[12]

That's the headline effect, but the overall outcome was that visualisation made a household five times more likely to do something (anything!)[13] – not forgetting that both the visualised and the non-visualised homes had audits, information, and a cold hard £500 in cash.

Digging a little deeper, the thermal camera visualisation created a raft of other one-off fixes, from improved glazing, to wall insulation, to fixing leaky doors, and to insulating lofts. But there were also continued behaviours that developed, like more diligent closing of windows and careful use of curtains.[14]

The thermal imaging seems to make energy more tangible – it 'rematerialises' the energy, says Sarah Darby from the Environmental Change Institute, Oxford.[15]

I see what she's saying

You'll believe it when you see it

Bryan Bollinger and Kenneth Gillingham of Stanford University studied peer effects in the diffusion of solar panels in residential areas. It seems that the diffusion isn't dependent on homeowners' desire to be green. They observed that: 'The geographic clustering appears to occur at both a zip code and neighbourhood level, and does not simply match the density or the "greenness" of the zip code.'[16]

These street- or postcode-level effects (their gravitational pull weakens further away than that) are discussed in relation to three factors: local marketing, social learning, and imagery.

Local marketing efforts are real, but are given a low effect-quality because they only affected behaviour when they were deployed, and deployment was sporadic and in smaller areas and shorter durations than the study. The times when they weren't deployed, or not in areas studied, make it likely that their effects are almost controlled for.

The interesting effects are social learning and imagery. The first is typically executed in the form of a solar panel installation contractor 'passed on' from neighbour to neighbour; personal recommendations are common in construction.

The last effect – imagery – is interesting. Most home efficiency improvements are invisible (cavity wall and loft insulation, boiler upgrades, etc.), but solar panels are obvious and serve as a big 'poster' for the work done. Bollinger and Gillingham suggest this 'image motivation' is a factor, and cite recent studies that chime with this thought by Lessem and Vaughn in Sacramento.[17]

Stephanie Simon in the *Wall Street Journal* writes: 'The problem, from a conservationist's perspective, is that much of the environmentally friendly behavior we engage in doesn't help set social norms because it's invisible to others.'[18]

But invisible sustainable behaviour only matters if non-sustainable behaviour is visible, because it won't be getting a fair crack of the whip. Stephanie Simon continues: 'What we tend to see, and perhaps envy, is the gleaming Hummer in the driveway, the huge flat-screen TV in the family room, the emerald lawn made lush by daily watering. (One exception: the recycling bin at the curb, which is now ubiquitous in many neighbourhoods.)'[19]

The visualisation of individuals' actions is significant in shaping our opinion of what is desirable within a group. This is as true of solar panels in US neighbourhoods as it is of the shaping of group ritual 40,000 years ago. To show just how strong the compounding influence is of each new installation, John Farrell, writing in *Grist*, interprets the data such that a tenfold increase in visible solar panels gives a tenfold drop in the time between subsequent installations.[20]

Synthetic images of the world around us affect our behaviour – like Chief Iron Eyes Cody surrounded by stack pipes and litter, cars queuing in a traffic jam, or a thermal image of our home.

Reality is equally potent – like the Texas car park strewn with litter, and a neighbour's solar panels.

But Trope, Liberman, and Wakslak give us a great summary from their work on construal levels: 'an abstract representation [like language] carries the essence of the referent object whereas a picture is a concrete representation that carries the properties of the referent object in full detail.'[21]

See what I mean? Asking with the right images is vital.

Can't see the wood for the trees

Chinese consumers use 45 billion pairs of disposable wooden chopsticks annually. At this rate, forests will disappear from China in twenty years. The Environmental Protection Foundation wanted to raise awareness of this waste. DDB Shanghai was commissioned. They are part of the global – and famous – advertising network.

DDB recycled over 30,000 pairs of wooden chopsticks and built a 5-metre-high 'tree'. It was broken, or 'chopped', in the middle. And displayed in Shanghai. The message couldn't be clearer, says Elaine Wu writing in the DDB blog: 'Stop and think of China's dwindling natural resources the next time you're about to use disposable wooden chopsticks!'[23]

But remember, the raw behaviour of others plugs that 'norm' straight into our brains without having to negotiate the cognitive assault course. And of course the message being delivered is a descriptive norm, not an injunctive norm.

The *real* message couldn't be clearer: 'So many people use these wooden chopsticks that there's more than enough to make a life-sized tree sculpture. They're everywhere. But you shouldn't use them. No. Not you. Even though there's so many of them. Look at them. Look away.'

We've ended up with our Texas dirty car park, where the injunctive norm (don't mess/don't chopsticks) contradicts the descriptive norm (abundant mess/abundant chopsticks).

So how could we fix it? We know the injunctive norm is more powerful than the descriptive norm, and we know that the negative of either is better yet. That leads us to a message somewhere around 'don't use chopsticks, few people use chopsticks'. We don't even need to say why, really. The visual 'drama' for this could be in the form of people eating with substitute chopsticks like pens, laser pointers, scissors (closed), hat pins, in a nonchalant way. Could be a TV commercial, a stunt in place of the tree, or an event in a restaurant. There are lots of ways of bringing it to life. But the point is to do it in a way that works.

A clever idea that evokes unintended behaviour is not a very clever idea at all.

Chopsticks, anyone?

4 Ask at the right time

'Not tonight, Josephine'

Music-hall song, Florrie Forde, 1876–1940
(often attributed to Napoleon)

Toyota Motor Corporation is famous for creating and implementing the Just-In-Time manufacturing system. Many see it as an extension of Henry Ford's production line approach, but this is not true. On the contrary, in 1956 Taiichi Ohno led a Toyota delegation to the production facilities of Ford Motor Company and General Motors. They saw large amounts of inventory sitting around in warehouses wasting space, and time, and money. Ohno was unimpressed, particularly as he was trying to find ways of setting up the Toyota factory to produce parts in a timely manner.[1]

All that changed during a visit to the Piggly Wiggly grocery store.

The first Piggly Wiggly grocery store was opened in the autumn of 1916, in Memphis, Tennessee, by the company's founder, Clarence Saunders. Apart from some unfamiliar brands and oddly low prices, it would not seem too dissimilar to today's stores: there were turnstiles at the entrance and customers would walk around picking goods from the shelves, returning to a 'checkout' with their selection. The now familiar process of having visitors wander around the store removed the need for assistants to serve-and-fetch for customers – this was revolutionary at the time. And the ease with which stock could be monitored, ordered, and refilled straight back on to the shelf without time spent in a storeroom was revolutionary – the store *was* the storeroom.[2]

This was the genesis of the Toyota Production System, which Taiichi Ohno often described in terms of the Piggly Wiggly supermarket. It was a pull system, driven by the needs of the receiver, rather than the conventional push systems driven by the needs of the producer. It has many times since been refined, and many times since been copied. (By Ford and GM, too.)

Is just-in-time delivery equally important for information? Yes. In its crudest sense, asking a question at the right time at least means it gets consideration.

In a more refined sense, if we have too many messages competing for our attention we can make seemingly 'uncharacteristic' choices – there's no beautifully managed steady and equal degradation in the attention afforded to inputs and a subsequently even reduction in the fidelity of our response. There's a cliff involved – one that we fall off.

And I'd like to explain why – using cake.

One slice or two?

Fruitful questions

In the late 1990s Baba Shiv and Alexander Fedorikhin, of the universities of Iowa and Washington State respectively, prepared an experiment where respondents had to remember something they were told, and then choose a snack.[3] It sounds easy – and, in a way, it is. The choice of snack is important, though. It was either:

1   a lovely, delicious, but unhealthy chocolate cake;
2   a healthy, crunchy, fresh fruit salad.

Under normal circumstances, they figured, more often than not the impulsive self would want chocolate cake, but the rational calm self would over-ride that choice and go for the healthy option. This was true. But they wondered what the calm rational brain would do if it was busy doing something else – like remembering a number?

They had the respondents walk one at a time from a holding room into the snack room. One group were given a two-digit number on leaving the holding room, and told to recite it to an official on entering the snack room. They could then choose a snack, privately. For the other group it was the same, except they were given a seven-digit number. What difference did it make?

- Less than 40% of the two-digit people chose the chocolate cake.
- More than 60% of the seven-digit people chose the chocolate cake.

Why is this so?

When we're processing information – such as choosing chocolate or fruit – our more rational, considered brain is involved. That makes sense. But if it gets a bit overloaded (by trying to remember a sequence of numbers) we don't deliver a steady degradation in the quality of effort we give our decisions, we outsource some to the (increasingly attractive) spare mental capacity available in the impulsive, instinctive part of our brain. And the impulsive brain reaches different conclusions. Ably illustrated by the increased choice of 'naughty but nice'[4] chocolate cake from the seven-digiters.

You can observe this effect over large groups of people, and in any combination of both sexes because there doesn't seem to be any gender bias. However, there is an attitudinal split: respondents who showed a pre-existing 'impulsive' attitude *collapsed* under the weight of the seven-digit phase, with over 80% of them choosing cake. But lash 'impulsives' and 'prudents' together in a two-digit phase so everyone gets access to their good clean cognition and everyone played nicely with only 40% of all types choosing cake.

Shiv and Fedorikhin conclude by saying, 'the characterization of the consumer in previous decision-making research as a "thinking machine," driven purely by cognitions, is a poor reflection of reality'.[5]

The reality is that if we don't allocate cognitive resources – if we 'act without thinking', in colloquial terms – we're more likely to make choices that have a strong impulsive appeal and a weak cognitive appeal. (There's a reason why the grab-bags of chocolate are at the till in a petrol station.) However, if we do allocate cognitive resources – if we 'give it some thought' – we're more likely to make choices that have a weak impulsive dimension but stronger cognitive appeal.

Adam Smith, author of the first modern theory of economics, *An Inquiry into the Nature and Causes of the Wealth of Nations*, calls this division the 'passions' on one hand and the 'impartial spectator' on the other.[6] It's more commonly referred to as 'higher' and 'lower' order thinking, or System 1 and System 2.

The 'lower' or System 1 brain is impulsive, intuitive, associative, and rapid in its response. It is interested in the immediate – anything in the future is irrelevant. System 2 is heaps more analytical. It's calculating and rule-governed. It's where we 'work things out' – use reasoning. We're much more considerate of future consequences.

Does the Shiv and Fedorikhin experiment mirror any experiences 'in the wild'?

In the USA, the School Nutrition Dietary Assessment Study-III collects data on school and student diets. There are two bits of feedback that almost exactly replicate Shiv and Fedorikhin's experiment: between 40 and 50% of pupils and staff commented on problems with noisy cafeterias, and pupils spent five minutes of their thirty-minute lunch break queuing.[7]

A cafeteria full of one's peers talking, banging and clattering, selecting tables, and making seating choices is a tsunami of stimulation for the senses. It's the 'seven-digit phase' made real. So if additional food-choices are available while the children are queuing – like handy snack-sized additions to a main meal – we could expect choice decisions to be handled by System 2: the impulsive 'us'. And if those choices are equivalents of fruit salad and chocolate cake, we can expect more of the latter to be chosen.

It raises rather interesting questions about the nature of free choice. Assume that the school board are incentivised to provide healthy food choices. Even further, let's suppose they have a mandate to encourage healthy food choice. The non-psychologically informed fight is usually between those that want to restrict non-healthy choice and those that want to have choice defined by the consumer (in this case the children through the choices they make, as that's what they want). Shiv and Fedorikhin's insight tells us these opposite sides aren't the only sides in play. It tells us to create a calm place to queue where decisions about additional snacks can be made by the calculating analytical brain – the 'impartial spectator' of Adam Smith's *Wealth of Nations*.[8] You can still choose cake, but you'd do so more knowingly.

It's an approach that's tricky in execution, but a much more engaging way to begin exploring solutions.

It's apparent that timing and context are closely related in terms of how we handle information. It's important to get it right – especially if you're communicating with car drivers.

Speed target

What if I told you we could make the US road fleet – that includes both private cars and commercial vehicles – over 14% more fuel efficient without changing the existing road infrastructure, without talking to any drivers, and without publicising anything, in any way?[9]

You'd think I was mad.

On America's roads – like most roads around the world – a speed limit is not a target. But what if it was? The US Department of Transportation issued a study from Texas where they fitted new speed boards on main streets that told drivers what speed to drive to guarantee every traffic light is green. They call it traffic signal synchronisation. 'SpeedCheck TrafficFlow Manager™ shows drivers the current "green light speed" of signals, acting to inform drivers that signals are synchronized at a specific speed.'[10]

And it was this traffic signal synchronisation that kept the traffic driving at more consistent speed, which reduced fuel consumption by over 14%. That's a lot when you consider the US vehicle fleet has lower MPG than most countries, so the absolute amount of saved fuel is high. But why do you get 14% saving without appearing to do much? Synchronisation informs drivers of speed 'in order to moderate acceleration'[11] – because acceleration is where the internal combustion engine is disproportionately inefficient. It uses much larger amounts of energy to accelerate than it does to cruise at a constant speed. (To compound this, a large amount of that inefficient acceleration is thrown away during deceleration in the form of heat through the brakes.)

However, excluding the financial saving of reduced fuel consumption, the benefits of reducing carbon dioxide output in this way are in the least attractive dimensions – they are not exclusively for me, and they are not noticeable immediately. Are there any more attractive, personal, and immediate effects? Yes. The green-traffic-light-synchronisation-signs also reduced traffic delays in the US Department of Transportation test by almost 25%.[12]

That's significant in a country where everyone drives.

Savings of both time and money permeate this approach: inexpensive to implement signage; reducing cost of driving to the individual; making immediate and persistent improvement of infrastructure; making immediate and persistent reduction in journey time for the individual.

In the absence of new infrastructure, inexpensively improving efficiency of the existing is worthwhile; especially in ways that negate the Jevons paradox that tells us increases in efficiency tend to increase (rather than decrease) consumption.

Reduced carbon food – delivered

In the UK, larger supermarket chains often have a home delivery service. You select and pay for your goods online and they are delivered to your home in a time-slot you request – from early morning to late at night, usually within a one-hour range. It's reasonably granular. For the supermarkets there's a logistical challenge, and also a logistical opportunity. But a challenge the supermarkets are well used to dealing with, thanks to Piggly Wiggly lighting the logistical touch-paper nearly a century ago.

The poser: if each van's deliveries can be made in one circular trip then the 'cost' of each delivery after the first is only the incremental cost of each subsequent trip. The opposite would be a single delivery on a single return trip from depot to customer's home and back.

But the grocer isn't choosing when people want delivery, so how do they create a choice structure for customers so they can happily choose to be efficient?

Ocado have the answer.

When customers have made their selection and payment online, at the end of the shopping process, they have the opportunity to select a delivery slot – this is the perfect time to ask this question. On this page, delivery vans that will already be near the customer's home are highlighted as the 'green' option. This helps customers who want to be more efficient be more efficient. But there are also elements of reciprocity and normalisation at work. Reciprocity, because Ocado have taken the effort to indicate the green times so customers can 'return the favour', while the provincial normalisation effect of the green times is in its indication of when people *who're like you* are receiving a delivery.

They're selling about £600 million of groceries per year in the UK, and their growth, says Tim Steiner the CEO, is 'limited only by our operational capacity'.[13] The more load they take, the more individual car trips to supermarkets they replace, thereby reducing the carbon dioxide cost of grocery shopping.

Trailing consumption on a rising tide

Creating distance between inputs aids cognition – Shiv and Fedorikhin left us in no doubt about that with their simultaneous digit-juggling and cake-selecting experiment. But in that case, and in the cases recently described, the timing solution has been proximate – interested only in creating near-term tightly choreographed sequential inputs where once there may have been simultaneous cognitive load.

However, the timing of information delivery is equally usefully examined where the gaps are wider. Years wider.

Harold Wilhite and Richard Ling examined informative energy billing in Norway in the mid-1990s. They experimented with the timing and content of electricity consumption on domestic bills for customers of Oslo Energi.[14] The standard billing procedure was four bills per year, three of which were estimates. They reduced the interval to 60 days *and* made sure it was a true reading rather than an estimate. It worked well.

They reported savings of 10%.

It's good. But it was bettered with the inclusion of trailing consumption: when bills were delivered with a comparison of the previous year and the months in-between (the 'trailing' comparisson), savings strengthened to 12%.

In contrast, advice and information made no impact on Oslo Energi customers. As recognition of the benefits of the trailing consumption billing, nearly eight out of ten customers wanted to continue after the experiment had finished. The Norwegian government also recognized the benefits, and made quarterly informative billing mandatory.

One could conclude from this example that a 'tree top' view gives a clearer reading of the world and how we relate to it. I don't know whether it makes our understanding objectively clearer (how can it if 'context' is the editor to the 'information's' author?), but it certainly changes the way we construct our understanding.

In a test of the perception of drought risk over time respondents in the UK were presented with an article about a drought in the USA and half were asked to imagine it was written the same year and half asked to imagine it was written fifty years in the future. When subsequently asked to comment on the likelihood of drought in the UK those that thought droughts seemed more likely far into the future were the same people who'd been asked to imagine the US drought article written fifty years hence. The reverse was true for the near-term article imaginers.[15]

It seems even known hypothetical adjustments to the calendar-scale (rather than to the clock-scale) make unknown changes to our perception of the world.

In a slightly recursive sense, this tells us that climate salience is high around events which are themselves climate created, and so that is a good time to talk about the issues involved.

However, the indicators of salience as a function of timing aren't always obvious. How do you spot them?

Best thing to do is ask someone – preferably a woman.

Gender cycling

Sometimes cycling is a good way to reduce the use of fossil fuel.[16] If so, communication designed to increase overall rates of cycling is better delivered at the right time – and it has nothing to do with a *bike-ability* index, a lot to do with infrastructure, and everything to do with observing women. More specifically, observing the proportion of women (versus men) who already cycle.[17]

That'll give you your tipping point.

Why? On average, women are more risk averse than men, and often bear a larger proportion of household shopping and childcare. So observing a large proportion of women cycling means the area is more likely to have developed practical, and safe, urban bike routes. For these reasons, women are the indicator gender, according to Jan Garrard from Deakin University in Melbourne, Australia.

You can see evidence of the indicator in parts of cities all over the world: in New York City only 25% of cyclists are women,[18] but in Central Park that rises to 40%.[19] In the Netherlands, which is full of safe, practical bike routes, over 50% of cyclists are women.[20]

If a government were thinking of a near-term cycling initiative while they were tackling issues of far-term private and commercial fleet adjustment, they'd be encouraged to find the conurbations at the cycling 'tipping point' by observing the proportion of female cyclists, and focusing resources – both informational and infrastructural – on them. Local not national is the watchword.

Taiichi Ohno – our Toyota production engineer – wasn't the only significant player in the development of the Toyota Production System. He was joined by Sakichi Toyoda – an inventor.

Years before working with Taiichi, in 1902, he invented a loom that stopped automatically if a thread snapped. It doesn't seem like such a significant invention today, but at the time it meant a single loom operator could handle dozens of looms at a time. And the end product would be guaranteed good. The reduction in defects and increase in output is something Sakichi would later use to help perfect the Toyota Production System.[21]

It's a shame we don't have an automatic loom shut down for our cognitive brain when it's overloaded. It'd stop the seductive impulsive brain getting to decide our fate (we might *want* our impulsive brain to decide our fate, but we can at least let the strategic 'us' pass on the decision knowingly).

There are lots of decisions to make about the broader timeliness of messages – like comparative billing or the salience of natural disasters – but it's clear that temporal consideration makes for better outcomes, whatever your criteria for success. Get timing right – whether in micro-sequence, seconds, minutes, or years – and you can be much more certain every pound, dollar, euro, yen, or tonne of CO_2 is creating the largest benefit.

Timely information, indeed.

5   Ask with the right incentive

'I've got these commandments'
  'How much are they?'
'They're free'
  'I'll take ten'

Incentives are obvious, aren't they? You just reward someone for doing what you wanted. Not so.

Joshua Gans is an economist at the University of Melbourne and the author of *Parentonomics*, so is perfectly placed to construct incentivisation programmes for his children. But when he tried to engage his children in lavatory training he found they 'gamed' the system in surprising ways.[1]

The incentive he gave to all his children was sweets. He created a sweet-based market for sitting on the lavatory correctly. He layered an additional incentive on top for his eldest daughter – guide your younger siblings to the lavatory, help them sit down when they need to 'go', and you'll receive sweets too.

His 11-year-old daughter gamed the system. Twice.

She managed to modify her lavatory visits so she went every twenty minutes throughout the day: three treats an hour, every hour. Eventually Joshua pulled the treat for this stunt. But his daughter had another eureka moment: 'I realized that if I helped my brother go to the toilet, I would get rewarded, too. And I realized that the more that goes in, the more comes out. So I was just feeding my brother buckets and buckets of water.'[2]

Her poor younger brother! However, as all of us are capable of, she figured out how to reap maximum advantage from the system at hand. It's the way of the world. But it's not always obvious what we think of as the 'maximum advantage'. And this is where asking questions with the right incentives gets more interesting than you thought.

(I'll bet you $1,000.)

Objects in the rearview mirror may appear closer than they are

Kelly Gallagher and Erich Muehlegger from Harvard looked at both tax and non-tax incentives designed to induce consumers to buy hybrid cars in the USA between 2000 and 2006.[3]

They had their work cut out to separate the strands of incentives. Some were local government designed and implemented sales taxes, others federal government designed and implemented taxes. Fluctuating fuel prices also played their part. And personal preferences were important to know and control for.

So they set about gathering fuel prices. They calculated car-use intensity in each North American State by using average travel times and population counts. They used per capita Sierra Club membership as a proxy for environmental propensity, and the deviation from the 100-year average temperatures as a proxy for climate change recognition. The proportion of military workers and casualties from Iraq and Afghanistan were used as a proxy for energy security sentiment. And they bought data on hybrid sales because it proved more accurate than vehicle registration data. They even separated private and government fleet purchases. They were nothing if not thorough.

And they found something rather strange happening with tax incentives – it seemed back-to-front.

Consumers intending to buy a hybrid were presented with a choice of discounts – either a sales tax waiver or an income tax credit. The average sales tax waiver was just over $1,000. The income tax credit was just over $2,000. You'd go for the two grand, right?

You're on your own.

For every consumer that took the $2,000 tax credit, seven took the $1,000 tax waiver. That's a big difference. Why? Gallagher and Muehlegger tell us that 'a sales tax exemption . . . is immediate and automatic at the time of purchase . . . an income tax credit . . . a consumer must . . . eventually collect as part of their tax return'.[4] But you still get the cash.

Why the rush?

We have a behavioural quirk called temporal discounting – we discount the future, so financial gains appear less attractive the further in the future they're promised.[5] The 'now' becomes disproportionately attractive. (Or, to mangle US automobile rearview mirror parlance, *objects in the present may appear more valuable than they are*.)

We draw a rather counter-intuitive tax incentive conclusion from this data: simply increasing a tax break doesn't automatically make a good more attractive. However, making a tax break more immediate starts to make it look very pretty indeed. In terms of a policy approach, Kelly Gallagher and Erich Muehlegger concur: 'immediacy and ease of tax benefit is a central attribute of any tax incentive meant to speed consumer adoption of energy efficient goods'.[6]

To give this some context, the sales tax incentive performs favourably compared with large-scale pricing mechanisms: Gallagher and Muehlegger estimate that 'a mean sales tax incentive of $1,077 is associated with an equivalent increase in demand for high-economy hybrid vehicles as a 26 percent increase in gasoline prices'.[7]

Has anyone taken this knowledge and applied it to the real world?

Israel has.

'Israel is one of the first countries to have signed a zero-emission agreement with the Renault–Nissan alliance. As part of this, the government has decided to reduce the tax levied on all new vehicle purchases from 80% to 10% for electric-powered models.'[8]

In concert with Renault–Nissan, Israel has implemented infrastructural and technological changes – such as building charging stations and switching the government fleet to electric vehicles – as well as communication and legislative changes that have helped raise public awareness and facilitate parking and toll road rebates.

They've made the juiciest incentive even more enticing – as *objects in the present appear more valuable than they are.*

Really rubbish games

Many Swedes return plastic bottles and cans for recycling. They receive a small payment. Noticeably fewer return glass bottles – perhaps because they don't get any money in return. How do you ask in a way that incentivises glass returns? Do you add a cash component to glass recycling (a 'pull')? Do you penalise for non-compliance (a 'push')?

Volkswagen run something called The Fun Theory,[9] which is a collection of approaches to behaviour change using 'fun' to drive engagement. They sought to solve the Swedish glass bottle returning problem in the form of a 'Bottle Bank Arcade Machine'.[10] It's a Heath Robinson marriage between a one-armed-bandit and a municipal recycling container – sturdy green plastic meets Vegas slots.

The recycling bin they use is free-standing, the width of two people, and stands at about chest height. It has six circular holes arranged in a line near the top designed to accept round glass bottles. It has a single light above each of the six recycling holes, and a pinball-style electronic scoreboard standing up above the bin at eye height.

One of the six lights above the holes would illuminate, and if the user pushed a glass bottle into this hole quickly enough, points would be scored. The digital scoreboard kept track of the overall score. The recycling bin also made characteristic arcade game noises.

On one evening 100 people used the Bottle Bank Arcade Machine, compared with two people who used the nearby 'normal' recycling bin. Not a peer-reviewed test, admittedly, but even so an impressive increase in recycling.

Cheap fun, surely.

Welcome to infinity, and beyond

A similar effort from The Fun Theory collection in Sweden is the 'Världens Djupaste Soptunna',[11] or the 'World's Deepest Bin'.

To paraphrase, they asked: 'Can we get more people to throw rubbish into a bin, rather than onto the ground, by making it fun to do?' The response was a standard waste bin in a public park rigged with all the necessary electronic equipment to express a cartoon-style sound of an object falling from a great height, triggered by every waste disposal effort.

This Världens Djupaste Soptunna collected nearly twice as much litter as a nearby undoctored litter bin (72 kg versus 41 kg).[12]

However, this seems to be less about encouraging use than it is about reinforcing use for those who engage: the unheard sound fails to 'prime the pump' as effectively as the Bottle Bank Arcade Machine. Having said that, park visitors who were engaged appeared to search for more litter once they realized disposal triggers the cartoon sound – some rifled thorough their bags to find more. This challenges the commonly held schema that litter bins are to be avoided because they are smelly and full of germs, and goes some way to creating a hyper-local norm of frantic litter-picking.

In practice, the bin creates unwitting Park Keepers of the participants by elegantly rephrasing the question 'Would you like to be on litter duty?' That's no mean feat.

In Berlin, Germany, they have aural bins too, except these ones say either 'Vielen danke/Thank you' or 'Welcome to Berlin' when you deposit an item of rubbish.[13]

Sepp Fiedler works at the company behind the idea. He says in conversation with CNN: 'The people like it. They pass them on the streets and start laughing because it's unusual to have this sort of contact with a litter bin'[14] – which is a perfect description of the schema-busting powers of fun and surprise that these talky-bins deliver.

Feel the pain – guaranteed

We work harder to avoid loss than we do to achieve gain.[15] This could be loss of time, or loss of social status, as well as the more obvious loss of money. This is embedded in an interesting business idea called Gym-Pact, which turns normal gym membership incentives upside-down.[16]

Geoff Oberhofer and Yifan Zhang sat in a Behavioural Economics class at Harvard. Professor Mullainathan taught them about our propensity to discount the future: the consequences of an action today motivate us more than future consequences. They used this knowledge to model the common problem of promising oneself gym visits but never going – watching a favourite TV show today and losing the benefits of fitness tomorrow is more attractive than missing a favourite TV show today for the benefits of fitness tomorrow.

This led to a gym membership model that charges you when you *don't* go, rather than charging you when you do.

In essence you sign up for the right to be financially punished if you don't stick to the workout schedule you agree in advance. By embedding loss in the immediate act of not going it neatly avoids the short-term benefit of watching TV instead, because the short term now has a cost. Also, the 'sunk costs fallacy' is dialled down: the traditional up-front cost of gym membership, that means you've paid whether you visit or not, is removed.

With this incentivisation model you're guaranteed to feel the burn; it just depends whether you want it in your wallet or on the running machine.

It's a lottery

Take speeding fines. As an incentive to drive considerately we're not asked the question efficiently, because we tend to discount the future.[17] Any financial penalty (speeding fine) for a desirable act today (speeding) will have to increase the further in the future it is levied in order to have the same effect. The same is true for future rewards of undesirable acts today – the reward (for not speeding) will have to increase the further in the future it is levied in order to have the same effect. Add to that our greater fear of loss versus our pleasure of gain, and it's clear that if you want to offer a future financial reward for performing today's undesirable action (not speeding) it has to be large – 'lottery winner' large. Can that be done?

Kevin Richardson's idea hit the jackpot.[18]

Kevin Richardson is a producer for MTV's Nickelodeon channel. His day-to-day work requires him to use, hone, and develop his storytelling skills – something he's familiar with and good at. He saw Volkswagen's Fun Theory call for entries and set about creating his solution to speeding.

'Each of us is the protagonist in our own life. So I wanted to put the single person at the center of this experience. But instead of . . . typical negative reinforcements [for speeding] . . . I decided to give this story a twist and positively reinforce them with cash for doing the right thing.'[19]

Good reasoning – but how do you execute it?

With the 'Speed Camera Lottery'. Kevin's approach is simple – those who are on or under the speed limit are entered into a lottery to win about £3,000 taken from the fines generated by the speed camera, with the 'entrance ticket' an automatically taken photograph of their car's number plate.

It neutralises temporal discounting by creating a winner's pot large enough to satisfy us with the potential future 'gain'.

Although (in a hushed voice) it does incentivise repeat drive-bys which will increase road traffic. It really *is* hard to ask with the right incentive (just ask Joshua Gans of potty-training fame).

Applying incentives is easy; understanding how they work, less so. Our instincts tell us we respond symmetrically. Temporal discounting tells us that's not true. Many of the examples here discuss financial asymmetry, including the real-life sales figures for hybrids where 'sales tax incentives . . . have a much greater effect on the demand for hybrid vehicles than income tax incentives which are delayed'.[20]

You have to look back thousands of years to find the roots of our asymmetry: we're hard-wired for a short and brutal life; a life where delayed gratification may mean no gratification; a life where the future is a distant place – be that next year, next week, or even five minutes from now. This ethos is even embedded in idiom: a bird in the hand is worth two in the bush; eat, drink, and be merry – for tomorrow we die. And up until the beginning of the Industrial Revolution, this was true.

Today, life in the West is not short and brutal – but we still tend to rely on those instincts. We want $1,000 now, even though it's not (rationally) the best offer; we want to get fit – but not today; we like talking wastebins and gamified recycling – they gratify immediately.

Asking with the right incentive makes a question inexpensive to ask, and equally inexpensive to accept.

That's good business.

Go far, but not fast

John Coleman is incentivised. At first glance, rather cleverly too. He's the Sustainability Director for Fayetteville in Arkansas, and has to find environmental savings in the city budget every year equal to his $57,000 annual salary.

It seems to make a lot of sense tapping into the old door-to-door salesman *on-target-earnings* approach.

But the incentive is skewed.

It's entirely rational for John to make savings up to – but not exceeding – $57,000 per year. He has no incentive to 'use' any saving he finds over that amount until the following year. For instance, if he found $570,000 worth of savings that could be sliced up into yearly increments, he could do that and retain his salary for a decade rather than deliver all the savings in one year.

Would it not be better to award an annual prize of $57,000 to the employee who makes the greatest financial saving related to the environment?[21]

A *highest-target-earnings* approach?

The signs are there

Some people can be quite inventive when trying to avoid loss – none more so than football fans in the Democratic Republic of Congo's capital city Brazzaville.

Football is a popular game in the DRC. Many people turn up to watch the games and dutifully pay the entrance fee. But those working on the entrance gates are poorly paid, and are quite happy to accept bribes to supplement their income. This happened until eventually nearly half of all gate receipts were effectively stolen in this way.[22] It had to stop.

The secretary general of Brazzaville's football league, Badji Mombu, had an idea.

He replaced the turnstile officials with teenagers who could neither speak nor hear. These deaf and dumb officials were thought incorruptible because football fans could not communicate with them.

Gate receipts soared. For a while.

But these new 'incorruptible' full-price tickets effectively meant money lost – and fans wanted it back. So some learned sign language. And as soon as the new turnstile officials understood they would be rewarded for selling tickets on the cheap, gate receipts tumbled by 30%

Effectively the Congolese government paid for a practical sign-language course targeted towards football fans.

It wasn't their intention, but it was very successful.

The writing's on the wall

Brazil has problems with graffiti. It's always hard to police, especially as the disincentive to do it – arrest – is a badge of pride in the tagging communities.

Local residents either pay to have graffiti removed (until the next time), or leave it there.

But one enterprising Brazilian offered a different outcome to the taggers via a sign screwed to their wall. It reads (translated): 'Dear Graffiteers. Please do not vandalise our façade. The money saved from repainting it is being donated monthly to institutions that help orphaned children and those who have serious illness.'

They have a clean wall, in a street where every other house is tagged.

Part II

The unexpected

Welcomed constructions with unexpected results, and unexpected constructions with welcomed results

Defaults are unexpectedly powerful tools for marketers and legislators: the town of Schönau in the southern German state of Baden-Württemberg shows us how.

Commitments can have an unexpected 'Jekyll and Hyde' effect. In short, they behave differently depending on when commitments are made relative to when they'll be enacted: the larger the gap, the more different the answer.

Defaults and commitments aside, sequencing of information is rarely considered in the construction of questions. But it can turn people off so violently they won't get anywhere near the content – particularly if you're talking about carbon. In fact, there's every suggestion that sequencing not only affects the outcome, it *is* the outcome – our relationship with happiness shows the way.

A Korean 'singing road' that aids speed-awareness is both obvious and obviously intentional – temperature cues that affect behaviour are neither. Even so, both approaches give delightful results, as do resistance light switches linked to energy prices.

Welcome to the . . .

. . . Unexpected.

6 Ask – but have a default option

'No one ever got fired for buying IBM.'

Unattributed

We're busy. Busy running a household. Busy working. Busy commuting. Busy running errands. Busy trying to find clean socks. Choice – especially mundane choice – we'd prefer constructed to be answered quickly and painlessly.

And this is where defaults come in.

We're surrounded by them: the height of a door handle; driving on the left; QWERTY keyboards. (The last, designed for early metal-and-ribbon-ink typewriters to keep commonly used letters apart to stop them from hitting each other and jamming the typewriter. An example of a default set for a machine's benefit, not ours.)

And not only are we surrounded by defaults, but we tend to stick to them: more people get divorced than switch bank accounts[1] – despite there being plenty of offers and products available and a financial penalty for sticking with a poor choice (bank accounts, I mean). In some cases defaults become conventions that are so important they are written in to law – which side of the road do you drive on?

Asking a question with an in-built default option can be more powerful than you might think.

German efficiency

Schönau is a small town of 2,500 people in southern Germany. Roughly 90% of the people who live there buy renewable energy to power their homes.[2] The average number of German homes with a renewable energy supply is 1%. It's a huge difference.

You might think it's because Schönau is full of environmentalists. You'd be wrong: it's a small traditional picture-box German town in the heart of the Black Forest.

You might think it's because there's a quirk of law that requires locals to sign up to the renewable supply. You'd be wrong: Europe has long had a deregulated power supply market available to any energy supplier, be they green, grey, or brown.

You might think it's because I misread the report. But you'd be wrong: it's approximately 90% versus 1%. Why the difference?

Defaults.

The default electricity supply to homes in Schönau is from renewables. That's it. It's as simple as that. The origins of this set-up, however, are anything but simple.

On 26 April 1986, the Chernobyl nuclear power plant had a melt down. Radioactive isotopes, blown into the air from the Russian disaster, spread all over Europe. They reached Schönau in Germany, where Ursula Sladek – a homemaker in her late-thirties – lived with her four school-aged children. They had to stay indoors for weeks to avoid danger. It was no false alarm – twenty-five years later, the wild mushrooms are still considered unsafe. At that time she vowed to find other ways to generate power, resulting in an audacious bid to take over the town's electricity grid.

It didn't go well.

And nor was it particularly popular. By a vote of 52% to 48% her consortium won the right to run the electricity grid. Even then they still didn't own the grid: that had to be purchased for 9 million Deutschmarks. It was, eventually.

So they set up EWS (Elektrizitätswerke Schönau) and set about purchasing mainly renewable energy, and selling it to residents of Schönau. Like all energy providers in Europe at that time, they had a monopoly of supply: there was no such thing as customer choice. It was only a year later that the European energy markets were liberalised to spur competition.

Energy providers across Europe – including the management of EWS – wondered what would happen to their customer base once markets were liberalised, especially as 48% of Schönau's residents voted against the consortium that went on to buy the grid and create EWS.

But nothing much changed: Nearly every customer stayed with EWS.

In experiments on defaults relating to electricity supply,[3] Daniel Pichert and Konstantinos Katsikopoulos, from the Max Planck Institute for Human Development, found that the *default option* always has the most customers whether it's green, grey, or brown electricity. This is clearly what was happening in Schönau.

Interestingly, the results showed little principled decision-making around electricity supply as only 2% of respondents criticised a green default as 'impertinent'.[4] (As an aside, it appears that if you want people to engage with a choice it may be better to remove defaults completely.)

The McKinsey Quarterly says in this regard: 'Defaults work best when decision makers are too indifferent, confused, or conflicted to consider their options . . . The default, however, must also be a good choice for most people. Attempting to mislead customers will ultimately backfire by breeding distrust.'[5]

Inconvenience, indifference, uncertainty, and lack of responsibility can create the stasis that leads to unchallenged defaults. Oddly, few people question the merits or otherwise of a default – possibly because of an inference that it's 'approved' by some sort of authority.[6] This tacit approval was found to exist in an organ donor experiment where organ donation was specified as a default state, out of which constituents would have to opt if they disagreed – participants inferred that policymakers were implying their willingness and recommendation by making it the default.[7]

Part of the 'stickiness' of defaults is to do with the endowment effect. Endowment creates a situation where we appear to value the things we own more highly than the things we don't, but is driven by the dislike of losing something we own. Loss aversion is an important ingredient. Endowment effect is usually in reference to things we choose for ourselves, but it does work even with things we're given: like a default – it's a 'pre-selected' ownership. Pichert and Katsikopoulos say: 'In a sense, the endowment effect and the effect of defaults are related because the default is what people are endowed with.'[8] (For more on endowment see chapter 16, 'Ask for it back')

'Asking' about electricity supply using defaults is about sustainable behaviour alone – not a definition of what constitutes sustainable energy. That will change as time goes on. But defaults can work as a component in creating investment flows towards new solutions. And like most things from the behavioural canon, it's near costless to enact, and is persistent in its effects. But there is a challenge inherent in defaults, especially for government: *quis custodiet ipso custodes? Who guards the guards?*

That's a challenge for all of us.

(As well as trying to find clean socks.)

Your mug

Starbucks™ – the coffee shop – will give you a 10% discount on your drink if you bring a reusable travel mug. It's designed to reduce the amount of disposable card cups sold. It's well meaning – or at least appears to be. But it's ineffective.

The default pricing endows you with a full-price option, from which you can consider a 'gain' of a 10% discount by bringing a travel mug. But we respond less well to gain compared with loss.

If they flipped the promotion on its head by reducing all drink prices by 10% and then *adding* that discount – a *loss* – back on to the price for those only able to use a disposable card cup, you'd get a much larger number of customers investing time and money exploring reuseable travel mugs.

Catering for a conference

The Behaviour, Energy, and Climate Change Conference experimented with conference mealtime default for delegates.[9]

In previous years they'd done what every conference does – prepared a chicken/beef/lamb/fish dish and offered a vegetarian option. And they had data: in the year before experimenting with defaults they tracked their delegate's tastes – 83% chose the meat-based option, and 17% requested vegetarian.

The following year they flipped their default for the meal: 700 people took their seats to find the default meal was vegetarian, and a meat-based dish was the option.

It was the same conference, with either the same people or people of the same type, year in, year out. Despite this their consumption pattern almost exactly flipped from the previous year – now 80% took the default vegetarian dish, and 20% requested the meat-based option.

It seemed as if they'd all changed their eating habits from one year to the next. However, diet choices are not taken lightly – vegetarians won't eat meat out of principle, and meat eaters often won't sacrifice meat out of choice.

That's the power of a default.

7 Ask for a commitment (in the future)

'da mihi castitatem et continentiam, sed noli modo'
(Give me chastity and continence, but not yet.)

Saint Augustine, 354–430

Odysseus was on a long, tough journey home to Ithaca after the Trojan War. Among the many trials and tribulations along the way, Odysseus and his men had to sail past the island of Sirens. The Sirens were bird-woman seductresses with songs so enchanting that any passing sailor hearing their refrain would be compelled to steer towards the shores of their rocky island and face certain shipwreck, and possibly death.

No sane sailor wanted to hear the Siren song.

Odysseus wanted to hear the Siren song.

But he knew he wouldn't be able to control his actions as soon as he heard them – and he knew his men couldn't control theirs either. Odysseus asked them if they would stop their ears with wax, and lash him to the mast of their ship. He gave them instructions to lash him tighter if he begged to be released.

As expected, when they sailed within earshot of the Sirens' call, Odysseus was seduced. He begged to be released. His men lashed him tighter and tighter, only releasing him when his expression turned from one of bliss to one of pain – at that point they were sure to be out of earshot.

They were. And they were safe: Odysseus had heard, and survived, the Sirens' song. They'd stuck to their plan.

We are all Odysseus to some extent: we make different decisions ahead of time compared to 'in the moment'. It's often better to ask for a commitment to a course of action ahead of time. Jack Fuller, a neuroscientist, tells us: 'Economists now recognise that we can prefer one thing in a low-stimulus (i.e. reflective) context, but in a high-stimulus (i.e. tempting) context, we act differently. This inability to stick to our decisions was once called "weakness of will". Today economists refer to it as 'time-inconsistent preferencing.''[1]

I'm sure that's what Odysseus would call it too.

Lashed to the mast

Dean Karlan, an Economics professor at Yale, came up with the idea of opening an online 'Commitment Store'. He'd done a lot of research on commitments and money saving (even naming the research paper after Odysseus and his 'mast' antics). Ian Ayres, Barry Nalebuff, and Jordan Goldberg – all from Yale – got involved in shaping the idea. Dean, Ian, and Barry founded a commitment business call StickK, and the website went live in 2008. It uses the commitment principle – amongst other things – to help us stick to promises we want to fulfil in the long term but find hard to combat in the short term.[2]

It works simply: you define a goal, lay some money on the line, find a referee, and designate some supporters amongst your friends to help cheer you on. Smoking cessation and weight loss feature heavily.

One of the founders, Ian Ayres, took his weight-loss commitment one step further by auctioning his right to gain weight on eBay. He explains it: 'The winner of the auction wins the rights to receive any forfeitures on my StickK weight maintenance contracts over the course of the next year.'[3]

Likewise, when the wife of James Hurman, a 30-year-old man from Auckland, New Zealand, was expecting their first child he decided to give up smoking – again. He'd not been particularly successful in the past so decided to sell his right to smoke. (He'd not seen StickK.com.)[4]

He had a lawyer write a contract penalising him over £500 for every cigarette smoked after his quit date. He published this contract globally. A fellow worker ended up buying his contract for about £150. There was no escape.

It worked. James quit smoking.

'I've quit many times in the past and found it difficult, exhibiting each time the usual symptoms of annoyingly persistent cravings . . . This time, however, the symptoms didn't arrive.'[5]

He suggests it might be the immediate financial penalty – which is large. It places his system 1 and system 2 thinking in turmoil but his immediate desire to smoke is beaten by his immediate desire not to lose over £500.

Lashed to the mast, and then some

'Mast lashing' can be found in retail stores in the form of shower-timers to help reduce water stress; some are the traditional 'hour glass' shape and full of sand, others digital, but all are waterproof. You commit to a duration in System 2 rational mode before showering, thereby attenuating the seduction of System 1 once awoken by the lovely warm shower water. (Incidentally, they work very well for children. They are less relevant in modern homes that use water efficiently.)

However, these devices are less effective at priming behaviour than they are at managing it once primed: following a drought in Queensland, Australia, many inhabitants bought a shower-timer because they'd seen first-hand the effects of water scarcity.

What else primes our behaviour?

Sirens sing many songs

Levels of construal appear to be recursive: the time at which an event manifests itself affects the language we use to describe it, just as the description of an event adjusts when we think it happened. (Or, as manipulations of construal affect distance perceptions, the distance of an event influences its construal.)[6]

Perhaps this chapter should be called 'Ask for a commitment (in the future – or ask for the future in a commitment)'?

Bit odd though, innit?

We've discussed construal on the temporal scale, but our 'inconsistent preferences' are present in other areas too – we also see its effects in issues of space, proximity to other humans, and our imagination: 'different dimensions of psychological distance (time, space, social distance, and hypotheticality) affect mental construal and these construals, in turn, guide prediction, evaluation, and behaviour'.[7]

Our description of events changes in four dimensions: 'here/not here', 'now/not now', 'me/not me', and 'clear outcome/not clear outcome'.

By way of a glove-box explanation of the 'me/not me' construal, if we're asked to describe reading a book in the near future we're likely to use terms like 'flipping pages'. If we imagine reading a book in the distant future we use terms like 'getting entertained':[8] The further away an event is, the more it's seen in a 'tree-top' schematic way; the closer an event, the more we see the 'trees' and not the 'wood'. (It is interesting that idiomatically we use and understand 'not seeing the wood for the trees'; we have an innate understanding that 'in the moment' decisions are different.)

More importantly, the 'self-truth' of decisions generally increases along with distance: 'participants' general attitudes were better predictors of behavioural intentions for distant future opportunities than for near future opportunities'.[9] As distance increases we tend to resolve conflict in favour of the values we each find central – the 'noise' of immediacy decreases.

Does clarity translate directly to 'better' decisions? It depends, actually.

It depends on whether we get the most benefit from the immediate, emotional, noisy decisions or whether we get the most benefit from the delayed, rational, calmer decisions: should 'going to the dentist' be lumped in with 'joining a health club'?[10] It seems fair from a distance, as they're both about health – and that's what participants in a test said when asked to imagine them in the future. But going to the dentist imagined *in action* was lumped together with 'getting a tattoo', because they both involve chairs and pain.

Which is correct?

They both are. But in most instances the delayed decision is the one where we see the long-term effects with the most clarity, and it's the one where most environmental resource-relieving choices make sense.

Ask for a commitment in the future.

Wax in your ears

There are two categories that are discounted similarly, according to Hardisty, Johnson, and Weber: finance and the environment. 'This is good news for traditional economic models of discounting which employ a single discount rate across domains.'[11]

The good news is that it is helpful for weatherisation and sustainable home improvements where the financial outlay can be pushed into the future by a 'Pay As You Save' scheme.

This is the basis of a UK government scheme where homeowners can apply for funding to pay for a range of efficiency improvements, including thousands of pounds worth of wall insulation or solar water heaters or panels. (There are some process challenges, not least of which is asking utility suppliers to be the source of loans, which requires the type of financial regulation normally only applicable to banks.)

The 'lack of upfront cost' is attractive, and we can construct a concurring factual using a temporal discounting approach to pension contributions which are delivered in the form of 'Would you designate part of a future pay rise to your pension contribution?' as described in Lynch and Zauberman's work on precommitment.[12] This structure neatly avoids the apparent pain of *losing* money already earned, as asked by standard pension contributions, by shifting the time frame. It also shifts the 'mental account' from which money is drawn. (We tend to have three main spaces: money earned/ potentially earned and not yet received; money earned and received; money saved. The reluctance to lose increases in that order.)

You can see how the Pay As You Save scheme can use the pension structure in the form of something similar to 'would you pay for efficiency improvements to your home out of money saved by those efficiency improvements?'

But while this form of future commitment may be seen as using a purely financial discounting scenario (perhaps unintentionally, perhaps not, but the process exists, however derived), that would underplay other dimensions of commitment involved.

Trope, Liberman, and Wakslak examined how our opinions of main and peripheral aspects of a product change depending on *when* we think about them more than *what* they are: 'participants thinking about the purchase [of a clock-radio] in the distant future expressed more satisfaction when the central feature was good and the peripheral one was poor (i.e., the sound quality was good and the clock poor)'.[13]

The central feature of the 'Pay As You Save' scheme is lower home fuel bills without any financial outlay. This is an attractive central feature.

Peripheral features for the majority of homeowners – like environmental responsibility and potentially better re-sell value of the property – are quiet support should they be called upon.

But why is it important for success that the system focuses heavily on the attractive central feature at the expense of the periphery? Because we're not all that good at distinguishing between central and peripheral features in relation to our homes: for instance, when making decisions about accommodation we tend to favour spaciousness over nearness to transport, because spaciousness is a more tangible aspect than commuting. However, in practice, we tend to get much more utility from shorter commuting than we do from spaciousness.

Temporal construal is central to the argument – everything else is on the periphery.

I'm Odysseus. No, I'm Odysseus.

In an observation of the trading of favours between two people – or 'logrolling' as they refer to it – Henderson, Trope, and Carnevale found that 50% of the pairs reached agreement about trades when the effects were in the near future, but over 90% reached a 'fully logrolling agreement' when trades' effects were in the far future. [14]

Who are we? *Who are you?*

You are all the things previously described, and subsequently summarised: we tend to discount gains more than losses, and of those we discount large outcomes less than small ones; [15] if the default is to receive something now we discount heavily (I want it now!), but if the default is to receive something later we're more sanguine;[16] we prefer sequences that increase over time rather than decline even with the same final outcome;[17] we like positive experiences to be spread out rather than get them all in one hit;[18]

In short, a rational schematic representation of the future plays against an emotionally charged visceral understating of the now. The reason is fascinating: as we get to weigh up the pros and cons of a choice, cons reduce their potency with distance, and pros do not – they are effectively dialed higher. Consequently a choice looks much rosier bathed in the light of the future shot through our calm, rational, calculating System 2 brain. (It is interesting to note that in any choice there are always pros, of which cons are a sub-set – without a pro you simply wouldn't bother going ahead so a con-only choice is effectively null and void.[19])

These things are all true. And the root of it all is temporal.

Of our logrollers, 'results showed that distant future participants approached the negotiation in a more global, structured manner than near future participants, leading to an increase in both individual and joint outcomes for the distant future participants'.[20]

Both individual *and* joint outcomes are better. That is significant.

And the quality of an outcome isn't swamped by weighty and complex issues, such as climate change, according to Dan Ariely. 'It turns out that big decisions are not very different from small decision[s]. In fact, when a decision is very big and very stressful and very complex, some of the irrationalities actually become larger.'[21]

That's why it's usually a good idea to ask for an undesirable environmental commitment on a future date – the practicalities and hassle of engaging (when it comes around) are attenuated, and the rational mind has a chance to interrogate the benefits on a more distal schema.

In other news, I'll go to the gym tomorrow, *definitely.*

(Or the day after.)

Both of your favourite movies

The two 'yous' are no respecters of age or taste. Read, Loewenstein, and Kalyanaraman asked people what movie they wanted to watch.[22] A simple question made more biting by asking them to pick a movie to watch immediately, and one to watch later.

The frothy rom-coms, blockbusters, and low-brow comfort films were picked to watch immediately. The more serious, cerebral, and substantial films were picked to watch later. The two 'yous'.

But what about beyond the laboratory?

Observations of Netflix queues show the 'serious' picks are left perpetually for later.[23]

8 Ask in the right order

裏には裏がある
(The reverse side also has a reverse side.)

Japanese proverb

Content is King, right? It doesn't matter if you say 'I need this, and I need that' or 'I need that, and I need this'. It's clear that you need two things (rather imaginatively titled 'that' and 'this'). They're the important bit. In fact, they're the only bit – the order in which they're requested has very little to do with it. Can't do. That would be silly.

Wouldn't it?

Most of us know a bit about 'anchoring' – even if we don't appreciate it as such. It's prevalent in supermarkets: we are offered food that's '75% lean', not '25% fat'. And it's prevalent in the medical profession: we prefer to talk about survival rates rather than mortality rates. (This is true of both doctors and patients.) It 'feels' wholly sensible, even though from a pragmatic point of view a 30% chance of death is the same as a 70% chance of survival, or '75% lean' is the same as '25% fat'. The order is important.

But our sequencing misunderstandings aren't solely the domain of numbers and percentages – linguistic and conceptual presentations can have their inferences camouflaged by the quirks of ordering.

If a monk asks of his superior, 'Can I smoke while I'm praying?', 'No!' would come the reply. 'Praying is a time for focus and contemplation.'

However, if a monk asks of his superior, 'Can I pray while I'm smoking?', 'Of course!' would come the reply. 'You can pray at any time – you will always be heard.'

Same question, different order.

Framing is practised in policy circles and used commercially on product positioning, but it's little discussed in terms of its scope, scale, and power – and rarely in terms of its execution.

So what is the right order? And why?

Driving backwards

Imagine a large pond that has a lily covering its surface. Everyday, the number of lilies doubles (each lily is the same size). If it takes 100 days for the lilies to cover the pond, how long does it take to cover *half* of the pond?

A lot of people are thrown by this question.

The answer is 99 days – if the lilies are doubling in size, their final 'doubling' must be when the pond is half covered. And a half covered pond can only exist the day before complete cover. Many people's instant reaction is to say 50 days – even if their rational brain ultimately works out the correct answer.

We fall prey to the instinctive answer because the world – in our experience – is full of linear relationships. We expect it to be so. If it takes a week to learn to play Chopsticks on a piano, Monday is bad, Sunday is great and somewhere on Thursday you're getting the hang of it. It's linear. Exponential learning would see you hopelessly stabbing at the piano keys on Saturday night as ineffectively as you were when you began on Monday morning, but by Sunday evening it would suddenly all come together. (If you stayed the course, that is.)

Our 'gut' reactions, or heuristics, aren't very good at estimating non-linear relationships.

This is the problem we have with Miles Per Gallon.

There are two ways of representing fuel used over distance travelled:
(1) miles travelled per gallons used;
(2) gallons used per miles travelled.

The difference is immaterial to the car, but unbelievably significant to our ability to judge fuel use. See if you can adjust for your gut reaction:

Which of these trade-ins saves the most fuel?

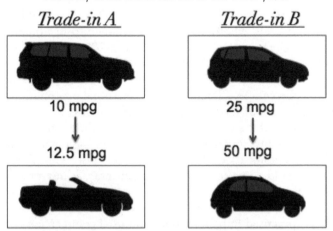

Trade-in A, from 10 mpg to 12.5 mpg, seems small – it is only '2.5' *thingies* better. Trade-in B, from 25 mpg to 50 mpg, seems massive – double the miles per *thingies*!

You've made a choice?

Hold that thought. You know this is a set-up in some way shape or form, right? Have I instilled some doubt? Are you're flip-flopping from one to the other? It's got to be 25 mpg to 50 mpg right? But how?

I shall ask the question again, but I will add *gallons per (hundred) miles* next to *miles per gallon*:

Which of these trade-ins saves the most fuel?

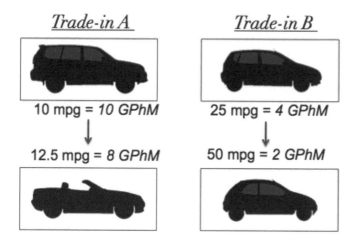

Both trade-ins save the same amount of fuel. I know – it was a trick question. We could've worked it out when we were shown only mpg but it's tricky because of those nasty non-linear relationships. We're much better with a straight up-and-down scale that has equal distance between measuring points.

And that's why it's instantly understandable when we switch the order to a linear GPhM scale.

The clarity GPhM provides leads us to an interesting conclusion: asking gas-guzzlers to nudge up efficiency can save the same *absolute* amount of fuel as stretching considerate fuel users up to hyper-efficient fuel users. As Ian Ayres and Barry Nalebuff write in *Forbes Magazine*: 'A typical car engine uses 1,000 times as much energy as a lightbulb, so conservation here is even more important.'[1]

A fact not lost on Eric A. Morris writing for the Freakonomics blog (at the time of his writing hosted as part of the *New York Times*) in August 2009 about the US 'Cash for Clunkers' trade-in policy. He tells us the average trade-in car was just below 16 miles per gallon (approx 6 gallons per hundred miles), but replaced by a 25 miles per gallon car (approx 4 gallons per hundred miles): 'A turnover of this magnitude has approximately the same impact as magically turning the average passenger car on the road into a Prius.'[2] Every 'clunker' that was 'cashed' is replaced with a car using over 2.5 gallons less fuel every 100 miles – for the rest of its life.

This fuel economy upgrade was as a result of 'free money' from the government, not as a result of consumer decisions based on clarifying the question of fuel economy by marking cars with the GPhM standard. But what if we did that too?

Let's stay with New York. There, State Senator Daniel Squadron has championed the use of gallons per mile over the traditional miles per gallon measure and has shepherded it through the Senate Environmental Conservation Committee: 'Gallons-per-mile is a common-sense, low-cost way to help us all understand just how fuel efficient your car really is. That's a win for the environment and a win for our wallets.'[3]

He is not alone. Urging the passage of the bill were the New York League of Conservation Voters, the Environmental Defense Fund, the Natural Resources Defense Council, the Sierra Club's Atlantic Chapter, and Senator Antoine Thompson, the Chair of the Environmental Conservation Committee – who says: 'This new method of "gallons per mile" as opposed to "miles per gallon" is an easier and more effective way of calculating the cost and efficiency of a vehicle.'[4]

For the millions of people who already own a car the comparison of fuel efficiency across models is no longer relevant. However, calculating the on-going cost of a vehicle is. And just as gallons per mile makes comparison clearer, so does it make costs clearer.

Say Ayres and Nalebuff: 'The problem is that miles per gallon doesn't readily translate into the dollar cost of driving. We don't say, "I plan to buy 1,000 gallons of gas. I wonder how far it will get me" Instead, we say, "I plan to drive 10,000 miles this year. I wonder how much it will cost me."'[5]

The order in which we frame data can have a greater effect on our interpretation than the data itself.

There's how you structure your question.

Wondering what your car does? Here's a handy table:

10 mpg = 10 GPhM
11 mpg = 9 GPhM
12.5 mpg = 8 GPhM
14 mpg = 7 GPhM
16.5 mpg = 6 GPhM
20 mpg = 5 GPhM
25 mpg = 4 GPhM
33 mpg = 3 GPhM
50 mpg = 2 GPhM
100 mpg = 1 GPhM

First impressions, last impressions

Peter Drucker, the great management thinker and *Wall Street Journal* columnist, tells us to 'do first things first – and second things not at all'.[6]

I might extend that to third, fourth, fifth . . . in fact, however many 'more' items there are – up to but not including the last on the list.

When presented with a sequence of events or groups of information we tend to remember better the first and last. This could be a written list, a chance meeting with someone, a conversation.

'Primacy' dictates those first stimuli are better committed to long-term memory because they are not crowded out by other events.[7] This effect is more pronounced the longer the gap between stimuli.[8] Additionally, if a sequence is to be committed to memory it is necessarily better rehearsed towards the beginning as a condition of rehearsal. (In some ways like the first mile of any car journey from your home, which is usually the same irrespective of the destination, and hence very familiar.)

'Recency' dictates that the most recent stimuli are waiting in short-term memory (only for a short time, evidently) and therefore have greater visibility.[9] Recency in slang terms is a sort of 'end of the list' bias. It skews our interpretation of all available information: it could be in the form of the last speakers at an event, or the last witnesses in a trial,[10] and can be a terrific challenge in a world with email and status updates continually pushed towards us.

'We pay a lot of attention to the most recent information, discounting what came earlier', says the behavioural economist George Loewenstein.[11]

You can only ask in the right order when you understand the effects of order on your audience.

Specifically happy, generally.

It was always thought in linguistic and psychology circles that the query order of two or more questions had an irregular effect on outcomes.[12] It was mostly ignored until experiments into its causes began the 1980s.

In *Nudge* by Richard Thaler and Cass Sunstein they refer to a 'happiness with dating' experiment; Strack, Martin, and Schwartz conducted it in 1988.[13] They asked only two questions. These were unrelated, and asked in the only two possible sequences. Oddly, the researchers recorded different results depending on the order in which they asked the questions.

If asked to rate 'happiness with life-as-a-whole' before 'happiness with dating', there was no real link. You could be happy or sad, dating or not, and it wouldn't relate in any meaningful way.

But if the order was flipped and respondents were asked to rate 'happiness with dating' before 'happiness with life-as-a-whole' the link between the two was almost 3.5 times greater: being in a relationship made you more likely to be happy.

Obviously, in this case the order is important. Or perhaps, even stronger than that, the order *is* the outcome.

But why?

'[R]espondents were more likely to use information about their dating-life in evaluating the quality of their life-as-a-whole when this information was more accessible in memory, due to its use in answering the preceding question',[14] say Norbert Schwarz, Fritz Strack, and Hans-Peter Mai as derived from their analysis of question sequences.

Our responses to question order can also be coloured by the relationship between 'general' and 'specific' questions. We deal with them in different ways. We tend to think of a general question as a request for a *summary* of a preceding specific question or questions.[15] This mistaken *summary request* is particularly pronounced after a sequence of similar-issue specific-type questions ahead of a general-type question – even in the face of instruction to the contrary.

There is a way to ameliorate the problem, though.

Schwarz, Strack, and Mai tell us how, 'when several specific questions bearing on different issues are presented . . .[they] are likely to draw attention to a more varied set of information, thus reducing the impact of any specific piece of information'.[16] In other words, jumble 'em up.

The order in which you ask questions is vital. Context, really, is everything.

Ordering tax

David Hardisty, Eric Johnson, and Elke Weber of the Department of Psychology at Columbia University were troubled by the fact that attribute framing is regularly cited, discussed, and exploited in government policy but an understanding of how to create it rarely exists.

In chapter 2, 'Ask using the right words', we talked in the 'Mandatory option' section about a 'tax/offset' semantic labelling test that ended with *mandatory carbon offsets* appearing to be a soothing balm compared to the salty irritation of a *carbon tax*, despite the same outcome of the labels.

With the same bunch of middle-aged male and female Democrats, Independents, and Republicans, they also explored 'query order'.[17]

To recap, they'd all read a sheet explaining how government policy would increase the cost of carbon intensive goods and services believed responsible for climate change, and told that the increase in cost would directly fund tactics to decrease the carbon expelled into the atmosphere by these goods and services, which had the same paragraph with the same word switch.

'The goal of a carbon [tax/offset], which may or may not be mandatory, is therefore to fund these efforts and ensure that the price of an activity reflects the true cost to society.'[18]

They were given the example of an aeroplane ticket. It had two prices: one was more expensive because it included a carbon tax; one was cheaper because it had no tax levied. All were asked to list positives and negatives for each. However, some were asked to list positives for tax first, and others were asked to list negatives for tax first. The list could be as short or as long as they wished.

The *only* difference was the order in which they listed.

Democrats and Independents were (generally) fine with this, whether they went positive on tax or negative on tax first: no drama. Similarly the Republicans were fine listing negatives first – 100% fully complied.

A test of reflection

Ordering significantly impacts our decision-making apparatus. Our decision-making apparatus is impacted significantly by ordering. (Just covering some ordering bases.) And to see just how much of an impact ordering can have, try Shane Frederick's *Cognitive Reflection Test*.[20]

When he worked at the Massachusetts Institute of Technology (he's now at Yale) he created a three-question test called the *CRT*, or *Cognitive Reflection Test,* as a measure of the strength of System 1's impulsive response versus System 2's planner-thinker.

And it's dastardly.

The word order has been fiddled with, so that the solutions are easily understandable when explained, 'yet reaching the correct answer often requires the suppression of an erroneous answer that springs 'impulsively' to mind', says Frederick. One of the questions you're familiar with, as it starts the 'Driving backwards' section – the question about lilies covering a pond. I've completed that answer for you.

See how you get on with the other two. Answers on following page.

(1) *A bat and a ball cost £1.10 in total. The bat costs £1.00 more than the ball. How much does the ball cost?*
    ____ pence

(2) *If it takes 5 machines 5 minutes to make 5 widgets, how long would it take 100 machines to make 100 widgets?*
    ____ minutes

(3) *In a lake, there is a patch of lily pads. Every day, the patch doubles in size. If it takes 100 days for the patch to cover the entire lake, how long would it take for the patch to cover half of the lake?*
    _99_ days

But when it came to listing the positives of a carbon tax first there was mutiny in the Republican camp – over 50% refused to do it at all. That request, in that order, did not compute.

Why?

We tend to appreciate the first value in a list as important relative to the others simply because it's first. In this test mutiny is assured because a Republican view of the world does not consider the first item in the list – adding tax – as important, indeed quite the opposite: removal of tax is a matter of principle. The (generally) ambivalent response to the query order shown by the Democrats and Independents is consistent with them showing little personal preference towards taxation.

Left to our own devices, we prefer to query – or 'weigh up' – the advantages and disadvantages of a choice in an order that feels natural – an order that conforms to our view of the world. Our biases are entertained. However, (excepting deeply held beliefs) it is possible for 'pros' and 'cons' order manipulation to force a non-natural consideration so as to accentuate or attenuate bias. Switching the 'endowed' belief to run against the grain of the naturally held belief can create a more neutral position from which to make decisions. The decision about what constitutes a neutral position is contentious and not part of psychology's consideration. However, observing the natural query order of a respondent and flipping it should attenuate natural bias, whatever that bias may be.

It does rather undermine the meaning of the common phrase 'get your opinions in order', though.

Any questions, communications, or discussions about carbon tax should begin with the downsides in order to involve everyone. If you want to talk about offsets, feel free to do that in any order you like. (It is important to reaffirm that this series of experiments are not an endorsement of tax as a disincentive. Quite the contrary, they equate tax with offsets in a way that embeds the cost of doing business into the consumer price. However, tax frequently appears in carbon debates as a behaviour change technique to be used *solely* to curb behaviour. Used in this way it is a rather brutal technique.)

As Hardisty, Johnson, and Weber say: 'What might seem like a trivial semantic difference to one person can have a large impact on someone else.'[19]

Answers

(1) *A bat and a ball cost £1.10 in total. The bat costs £1.00 more than the ball. How much does the ball cost?*
  __5__ pence
  The instinctive response is 10 pence, because it's a quick slice of £1.00 and £1.10.

(2) *If it takes 5 machines 5 minutes to make 5 widgets, how long would it take 100 machines to make 100 widgets?*
  __5__ minutes
  The instinctive response is 100 minutes as it follows the same numeral sets.

(3) *In a lake, there is a patch of lily pads. Every day, the patch doubles in size. If it takes 100 days for the patch to cover the entire lake, how long would it take for the patch to cover half of the lake?*
  __99__ days
  The instinctive response is 50 days as it's half of 100, and it seems like that's what we're being asked.

9　Ask kinetically

Perhaps sign language is the first thing you think of when it comes to communicating with movement. It is a good example, but it's not the only way. Texture is similarly overt and physical. And temperature must be included especially as we rarely – if ever – recognize its influence on our behaviour.

But is temperature really kinetic? Yes. When we refer to the temperature of an object we are simply recognizing energy transferring from one body to another – between our finger and the object we poke, for instance. If the object is warmer than our finger, energy passes from it to us: it feels hot. If the object we touch is cooler than our finger, energy passes from us to it: it feels cool.

Asking kinetically enables us to present information in often-unused forms – and that allows us to ask questions in often-unused ways.

Let's get moving.

Fight the power

When they were students at Stanford University, Peter Russo and Brendan Wypich designed a light switch with varying levels of movement resistance when switched on or off.[1] It could be configured to respond to a variety of conditions through this movement resistance: responding to user-load on the national grid (and by implication, the price of electricity); responding to the load within the neighbourhood; responding to a household-specific energy consumption goal. This use of haptics – or tactile feedback – is an often over-looked element in user experience.

It's a shame because, of the five senses, touch is the only one capable of simultaneous input and output.[2]

However, it's not particularly granular – in fact it's pretty crude in some dimensions. And it's only available at the point and time of use. But these don't need to be downsides. The simplicity is a benefit. And of course its use isn't tied to a light switch – other powered objects can take this mechanism. And if smart grids become more popular this is an interesting way for that grid to pass information to humans.

Touching.

Tactility aside, feedback on energy consumption at the point of use is not necessarily new. A few years ago French designer Alexandre Tonneau entered the Samsung Young Design Award with a light switch that illuminates with an intensity proportional to the amount of energy being consumed in the home.[3]

By making the cost of use immediate we're less able to 'discount' it as much as we would if it was kept as a future cost. It nags at that loss aversion quirk of ours.

It's a bright piece of communication, as are the Proverbial Wallets.[4]

Exhibited at Arts Electronica 2009, and written about in publications all over the world, the Proverbial Wallets are a Massachusetts Institute of Technology tangible interface demo from John Kestner, Daniel Leithinger, Jaekyung Jung, and Michelle Petersen.

They developed three wallets that kinetically communicate three aspects of an individual's finances: one vibrates when a transaction is processed, a second has a resistance-hinge linked to budget goals, and the third swells and shrinks to reflect the balance in an account. Making physical an abstract concept such as money is useful – it makes it immediate, denying a distant construal so that we literally feel the effects of spending. The DataBot from a young designer called Jan Barth is similar. It's a mouse that subtly and proportionately retards the user's movement when click-and-dragging files according to the file size: the greater the amount of data in the file the greater the amount of resistance when dragged across the screen.[5]

Kinetic communication is able to make the abstract immediate.

Bumped

We all have more expertise with kinetic communication than we might think: it's certainly true for those of us who drive.

In newer cars – internal combustion, hybrid, or electric – we see increasing amounts of driver aids. A popular one is the 'lane drift' type warning system, usually delivered through wing-mirror mounted cameras (and rather a lot of complicated trickery). But lane drifting needn't be 'asked' for by complicated in-car camera systems. A lower-tech version is the rumble strip on UK motorways. It only exists between the slow lane and the hard shoulder; serving as a kinetic reminder of correct road position (or lack of it, more importantly).

Textured paving is used to define boundaries between roadways and cycle lanes in countries all over the world. It's very popular in the Netherlands – but seen in Finland and the UK too, amongst other countries. Indeed, nearly a quarter of a century ago the UK's Traffic Advisory Unit worked to provide safer routes for cyclists by investigating ways to cater for the needs of the blind and partially sighted when using shared walking and cycle routes. Their solution was textured paving slabs that were marked in continuous ridges in the direction of travel for cyclist, and marked perpendicular to the direction of travel for pedestrians.[6]

Communicating through the feet of blind people (and sighted people too, of course) is not the first place many people go when asked to construct communication that identifies the demarcation between two points: a far-sighted solution for sure.

The use of traverse strips opens up some interesting possibilities beyond pedestrian and cycle routes. Both Ghana and the Philippines use them to slow traffic at intersections by having rumble lines get closer together approaching a stop sign: Ghana reporting drops in traffic accidents in the tens of percentage points for what is a very successful piece of kinetic communication.[7]

Some enterprising people have used this principle to create some rather surprising outcomes.

Running through the middle of the Hokkaido prefecture at the north end of Japan is Highway 272. It weaves from the coastal town of *Kushiro* through the mountains to *Shibetsu*. Near Shibetsu, the Hokkaido National Industrial Research Institute worked with Shizuo Shinoda to design a 175 metre 'Melody Road' that produces a recognizable tune when drivers travel at 28 mph.[8] Ostensibly a traffic calming attraction, it has been written about and awarded in international communications competitions.[9] It is a great alternative to a numerical static speed sign that also helps shape a smoother driving style, reducing fuel consumption in internal combustion engines.

The first example of melodic road markings was the Asphaltophone, created in 1996 by two Danish artists – Steen Krarup Jensen and Jakob Freud-Magnus – in Gylling, Østjylland.[10] It was not intended to communicate anything specific other than the melody. An art piece, really. However, the 2006 'Singing Road' in Anyang, Korea takes this idea one step further by singing 'Mary Had a Little Lamb' when driven over at normal speed in an attempt to keep tired drivers awake.[11] It would get my attention.

And it beats the 'Tiredness Kills' road signs hands down.

Staying with roads and driving, the Gregson Street railroad trestle in Durham, North Carolina, could use a 'Singing Road' – one that plays 'Stop (in the name of love)', perhaps.[12]

Why?

Spanning the road is a railway bridge. It is uncharacteristically low. The 'uncharacteristic' part is because most traffic flows freely apart from non-articulated trucks, which are typically used by self-haulage hire companies and driven by inexperienced drivers. Who among them would know that 11 feet 8 inches is a non-standard height for a bridge and *just* too low for hire trucks?

More than twelve drivers per year certainly didn't know.

It's such a problem that the rail company who own the bridge has installed a steel girder across the road just in front of the bridge so oncoming drivers who don't see the height signs hit the girder instead of the bridge – it's a lot cheaper to replace the girder than close the bridge.

'Singing roads' aside, what the owners of the Gregson Street trestle bridge haven't done is copy the example of some clever folks in Griffin, Georgia, who have the same problem. They've suspended a sign above the road a short distance from the bridge bearing the message 'If You Hit This Sign, You Will Hit That Bridge.'[13]

A kinetic sign, indeed.

Warm feelings

A rather obtuse definition of kinetic communication admittedly, but warmth – or lack of it – is the energy transfer from our body to the world around us, or from the world around us to our body. It's what we recognize as hot, and cold. But very few of us would recognize it as 'yes' and 'no'.

We should.

Often we colloquialize other people's attitudes along temperature lines – we say someone is 'warm' and friendly, or 'cold' and standoffish. Lawrence E. Williams and John A. Bargh of Yale wanted to see if there was any truth in this, so they concocted a way of testing the effects of temperature on our judgment of others.[14]

As part of their experiment Lawrence greeted volunteers and took them to meet a stooge called Randy. During the slightly awkward journey from meeting point to Randy's room, Lawrence nonchalantly gestured for the volunteer to hold his drink so he could more easily write down their name and particulars: sometimes the drink was a hot cup of coffee in a paper cup; sometimes it was an ice-cold fizzy drink.

When the volunteers reached the room under Lawrence's guidance they spoke with Randy about his life and education: he was initially a stranger to them. After their chat Lawrence took them away and asked them whether they would hire Randy as a project manager. They repeated this procedure exactly with each volunteer, except for alternating the drink as hot or cold.

Did it matter?

The warm-coffee-holders said positive things about Randy, including that they would be likely to give him a job as a project manager. You'd expect this because we all say nice things about strangers – don't we? Let's not be too hasty. The ice-cold-drink-holders seemed to be less accommodating – none of them said they'd be likely to give Randy a job.

A stark result.

Lawrence and John tried another angle. In a new study they asked participants to evaluate a therapeutic pack. The pack was either heated or frozen – either way, as a 'thank you' for the evaluation, the participants were asked to accept either a gift for themselves or a gift certificate dedicated to a friend of their choosing. The hot pack evaluators tended to dedicate a gift certificate to a friend. The cold pack evaluators were much more selfish and most took a gift for themselves.

A similarly polarised result, which leads us to conclude that temperature not only affects how we evaluate others (poor Randy), but also how we act towards others (poor friends).

I understand and accept this information, although I am drinking a hot cup of coffee so I wonder if I'm being more accommodating than usual? Perhaps I am. As Yoona Kang says, 'temperature priming . . . offers new insights into the ease by which incidental features of the physical environment can influence human decision-making, person perception, and interpersonal behaviour'.[15]

Kinetic communications really does allow us to ask questions in often-unused ways: the overt ways, like the road patterns and product feedback, are mostly sympathetic to cognitive load; the covert ways involving temperature do not have an off-switch, so impact behaviour whether they're acknowledged or not.

These are good signposts for asking questions kinetically.

The sign language at the beginning spells 'I cannot do sign language', which you might find handy, if not a little recursive.

Part III

The contradictions

Contradictory approaches make forceful claims – but behaviour change is always the winner.

There's this joke. In it, three people are travelling in a car. One is an automobile designer, one a mechanic, and the third a computer programmer. The car breaks down. The driver pulls over. They each offer an approach to the problem characteristic of their experience. The automobile designer asks for the handbook from the glove compartment to check the fault-finder. The mechanic insists they 'pop the hood' and delve around in the engine bay. The computer programmer simply suggests they all get out of the car – and then get back in again.

It's a great example of how we navigate life unaware of competing views: this section pits them against each other.

For instance, it's correct that legislators and marketers strip messages to the bare essentials – we have a 'finite pool of worry'. Argentine farmers and La Niña tell us that. It's equally correct to add options: the existing incorrect theory of cannibalization of market share tells us that. 'Magnetic' beer is our proof.

The final contradiction involves real and fake authority. We have trouble recognizing its authenticity, and so respond equally to either.

Sometimes.

I'm sure you'll love/hate The Contradictions.

10 Add options

'Sacco vuoto non può star in piedi.'
  (An empty sack cannot stand upright.)
                    G. Torriano, *Select Italian Proverbs* 90 (1642)

The effects of adding alternatives to a menu of choice are something both business and government underestimate, and often misunderstand. The most common assumptions are:

1   If marketers add a similar product to an existing range they expect it either to do nothing, or to cannibalize existing market share.
2   If a new candidate is fielded in an election the existing candidates expect her/him either to have no effect or to cannibalize existing voter share.

In other words, it is assumed that the addition of a new alternative either does nothing or sucks interest away from a member of the original set.[1]

This assumption is simplistic, and wrong.

The addition of an alternative choice can make an existing member more attractive.[2] This is counter-intuitive. And it violates the 'cannibalization' assumption – which is the minimum condition of most choice models. If we were rational actors in a rational world, this absurdity wouldn't happen. But we're not, it's not, and it does.

Adding an option does a lot more than just 'adding an option'.

Beer and cars

Joel Huber and Christopher Puto, of Duke University, USA, asked a simple question common to many all over the world: 'Fancy a beer?'[3]

It sounds simple.

Huber and Puto recruited over one hundred respondents and gave them a simple hypothetical choice: would you buy a beer that's $1.80 with a quality 'score' of 50/100, or a beer that's $2.60 with a quality 'score' of 70/100? Pay more, get better. Simple.

The choice saw 30% choosing the $1.80 beer, and 70% wanting the quality beer. (They obviously like the posh stuff.)

But here come the additions.

A low-quality 'decoy' at $1.60 with a 30/100 quality was added. No one chose it – not one. But it changed the desire for the original beers: With 0% wanting the $1.60 decoy, instead of a 30/70% split for the original beers it now shifted to a near 50/50% split. How odd. Rational actors in a rational world would not have changed their minds based on the addition of an unwanted outlier, and most choice models don't allow for this.

Does it work at the other end of the price spectrum? They tried a high-quality decoy at $3.40 with a quality of 75/100, and 10% chose it. Obviously (or so it seems), there were a few people for whom the original highest-price $2.60 choice was not high-quality enough. But the rest of the choice shift was phenomenal.

With the addition of the $3.40 decoy (which 10% plumped for), absolutely no one wanted the original $1.80 beer – despite 30% originally preferring it – leaving 90% climbing up to the $2.60 option. So instead of a 30/70% split for the original beers it now shifted to a 0/90% split.

The addition of options twisted the original choice: the decoy effect is powerful.

This understanding of choice architecture is at odds with how a traditional marketing campaign would approach the challenge to increase the desirability of a particular beer. In-bar one might see Buy-One-Get-One-Free, Happy Hours, etc. Out-of-bar you could see anything, such as posters and press adverts, up to and including TV advertising. That type of marketing effort costs money, and – even if it is successful in changing preference – the behaviour tends to 'flop back' once the marketing effort ends. It's highly likely it would have to fight the seemingly insignificant things like menu presentation and the associated decoy effect.

The question is, why not start there? (And maybe even leave it there?)

Huber and Puto put together a more complex test involving three base choices, each with three dimensions. It returned similar results. They offered three car choices, where acceleration, handling or fuel economy was equal to, or better than, the others in at least one dimension. This meant there was no clear 'winner', but there is a middle(ish) option for each dimension. The addition of a fourth car – a decoy – with superior handling criteria created a new 'middle option' car of what was one of the outliers. The respondents referred to this new 'middle option' car in interviews as the 'safe', 'compromise' alternative.[4]

To package this data up as a rule-of-thumb, they expected something in the region of a +10% increase in preference (sale, votes) for a target choice when a decoy was added.

But why does the centre of gravity shift?

It is possible respondents are working hard to minimize regret – if you define 'regret' as the distance between the selection made from the choice available and the perfect choice (for you): choose the middle (of three) and you insulate yourself from maximum regret.

It seems adding a new option shifts desirability which may allow differences to be more closely examined: 'when people cannot decide between two front-runners, they use the third candidate as a sort of measuring stick', says the *Washington Post* about election candidates.[5]

Dan Ariely uses an example of the 'third candidate measuring stick' with a Paris/Rome conundrum, in which an all-expenses weekend trip to Rome is played against an all-expenses weekend trip to Paris. They are different enough to present a challenging comparison. But with an additional 'decoy choice' of an all-expenses weekend trip to Paris *excluding* breakfasts, a closely related pair is created on the Paris side. Therefore, the choice between the inferior and superior Paris options is less challenging than either compared with Rome. Because of this, the superior Paris option (all-expenses weekend including breakfast) usually wins in this scenario because it is the best choice of a dominant related pair. (Equally, you could adjust for Rome instead of Paris and create the opposite dominant related pair.)[6]

The ability of differences to be more closely examined with related pairs is given credence by the cost-of-thinking approach. It states that decisions between closely related pairs (Paris with/without breakfast) are preferred because they charge a much lower cognitive 'cost' to work out than decisions where pairs aren't related (Paris/Rome).

We prefer economy of thought, in other words.

A lot of modern software-as-a-service businesses use decoy pricing. They might offer a similar price and package for a twenty-user-option as they do for a ten-user-option, and only a small price drop to the lowest one-user-option package, for instance. This lowest option seems like an outlier, and makes comparison between the two other options seem easier. Of course it does; it is 'Rome', it is the 'cheap beer' – it is the decoy option.

Restaurants are not to be left out. The addition of an expensive meal on the menu allows the other prices to creep up while still seeming like good value. (How many times have waiting staff heard 'I'll have the second cheapest bottle of wine, please'?)

It's an easy leap to make to use decoy effects to shift perceptions about the private and commercial vehicle fleets. The ability to massage the perception of hybrid, fully electric, or low-mileage vehicles is easy with decoys. Huber and Puto – of the 'beer bottle' experiment – wrote this suggestion, along with John Payne, in a study of the decoy effect in relation to selling cars: 'A manufacturer of cars with a relatively poor gas mileage (e.g., 20mpg) might decrease the effect of this dimension by first showing prospects a high-powered car in the showroom with much worse (8mpg) mileage.'[7]

Context-dependent preferences can easily be used to ameliorate our effect on today's resource-stressed world. It would work. It's persistent. And it's fairly inexpensive.

Sex and money

Adding options does force recalibration, but needn't be the exclusive province of the decoy effect. Adding options can be simply about presenting a normative balance.

In a study of UK schools, lack of access to information about safe sex was not a problem: there was plenty of it, and it was plentiful. But many authorities recognized the feelings of awkwardness for young people around the prevalence of sexual activity in relation to oneself, and around reactions of young people when asking sexual partners about contraception. Dealing with these challenges was considered essential to stop one of the most dramatic consequences of unsafe sex – unplanned pregnancy, and possibly parenthood. They even went so far as to invite young parents who had had unplanned pregnancies as teenagers to talk to teenage students about their experiences.

Understanding the consequences of actions is something teenagers commonly grapple with as they approach adulthood, and this seems like a good way to dramatize the possible consequences of unprotected sex.

Except, it isn't.

The UK government Cabinet Office and a think tank – The Institute for Government – explain it thus: 'the local practice of having previous teenage parents come and talk . . . helped them imagine themselves in that situation (Salience), made it seem more normal (Norms), and the young mothers themselves seemed rather impressive and grown-up (Messenger).'[8]

After some research they changed their approach by adding young people in their early twenties who had life experience other than teenage parenthood. This time the panels provided a more representative view of the lifestyles available. 'A typical panel of 20-something ex-students had three who were not parents, of whom one was recently married, one was in a long-term relationship, and one who had recently broken up. The fourth was also recently married and had just had a child. The fifth, on some of the panels, had been a teen parent.'[9]

As is often the case with young people, they were all articulate and impressive, and made concrete the consequences of a choice. But it was the systemic change that allowed the presentation of a more representative sample, as most people who leave school do not become teenage parents.

'Adding options' can create a more representative choice architecture, but they were adding options only within the category of 'lifestyles available to teenagers'. Sometimes this is a good choice. But a category alone does not always scribe the limits of choice for additional options. Sometimes available choice can extend beyond the immediate category. And many times, should. Especially when we're dealing with money, because its abstract nature really screws with our ability to evaluate opportunity costs.

'If I buy this Toyota, I can't buy a Honda.'

Dan Ariely and his team went to a Toyota dealership and asked visitors what they thought they would be forfeiting by buying a Toyota.[10] The team assumed people would have an answer for this question. Some said they were forfeiting a Honda for a Toyota – but many were caught offguard and a little shocked, saying they'd never really thought about it. The true opportunity cost of buying a Toyota was not being considered.

This is quite common.

True opportunity cost is broader than the category (Honda versus Toyota) and has effects extending into the future. Ariely says that consumers in the Toyota dealership were not saying 'in the future, I will have to give up two weeks of vacation and 70 lattes and 1,700 books',[11] even though they would make more informed choices by considering this. (Not different choices necessarily, but more informed choices certainly.)

I say you can go even further by considering future goods: your child's education, healthcare, time off, etc.

This raises some really interesting questions around our recognition of inter-generational equity (the notion of fairness across generations measured in economic, psychological, and sociological terms) and our collective understanding and response to the price shifting that is likely to occur if the cost of carbon dioxide and other greenhouse gases are directly or indirectly levied by the market or by the government on the products and services we use. (For instance, CRC, Wal-Mart, P&G, and Unilever measuring carbon load on their businesses and their suppliers.)

To go high end – and specific rather than general – for a moment, imagine the potential purchaser of a £100k petrol sports car feeling suffocated and angry at a situation where the cost of oil shoots up and/or legislation and carbon taxation starts to bite. Substitution may now occur. And will probably follow the 'Toyota–Honda effect' by staying within the category of fossil-fuel sports car, necessitating a downshift to a smaller (say) £70k model to reduce running costs or stay with the £100k model and take the extra cost on the chin. Both choices look, feel, and seem oppressive. They are. But even a tiny nudge to expand the available option with the next-door category of electric cars, which contains the £100k Tesla sports car, ameliorates the effects somewhat. And then adding consideration of opportunity cost over time means the £100k Tesla option also contains all the same tangible and non-tangible future goods (your child's education, healthcare, time off, etc.) that the £100k petrol sports car did *before* the cost of oil shot up and/or legislation and carbon taxation started to bite.

The equity created there is twofold: private cash and public good. Private cash saved is equity that can be spent or saved, and the public equity is in the form of reduced carbon dioxide emissions, which is by default passed to following generations, thereby delivering an inter-generational component.

We've got options. We just need to make sure we're not blind to the options.

Our gut responses to choice architecture are manipulated by 'adding options'. And I say 'are' manipulated rather than 'can be' manipulated, because it is happening whether we acknowledge it or not. As William Poundstone, the American author of *Priceless: The Myth of Fair Value (and How to Take Advantage of It)*, says of the beer price experiment: 'The Huber–Puto experiment is now a classic of marketing science. It shows that, in many contexts, consumers really don't know what they want and can be manipulated by the way a choice is presented.'[12]

That's a pretty stark statement.

If we're on the receiving end of a choice structure, can we immunize ourselves? Not really. But Shankar Vedantam of the *Washington Post* does offer this advice: 'Don't let salespeople tell you what issues to care about, and don't let candidates define one another. More simply, think for yourself and be wary if a difficult choice suddenly feels simple.'[13]

As a constituent, or consumer, I would add that one should play with the choices on offer to get a fairer reading – make imaginary substitutions, and change some of the parameters of the choices available. Also, expand the set from which you draw conclusions – the opportunity cost of a choice may be wider, more varied, and less bound by time than you may think.

Of course, if you are constructing choice (and if you're reading this book then the likelihood is that you are, or do, or will) measured by its success in reducing stress on natural resources, you can go some way to ameliorate the pain of reduction, or sell your option more readily.

That's an option to add, for sure.

Bin there

Unintended consequences are the bugbear of the well intentioned. All over Singapore – from the tourist areas to social housing estates – recycling bins are a common sight. They're an important part of the National Environment Agency's (NEA) commitment to increase recycling from +50% to 70%.

But there's a problem.

The recycling bins frequently contain food waste, which renders *all* of the contents unrecyclable. The *Singapore Straits Times* investigated eighty recycling bins near their office and found non-recyclable waste in all of them.[14] It plays havoc with the targets, and wastes the social capital expended by those who do bother to recycle. There's obviously a problem.

The National University of Singapore (NUS) has a solution.

Marcus Tay Guan Hock, the Sustainability Executive at the NUS, wrote in to Nudgeblog.org to explain that they solve this problem by 'pairing every set of recycling bins with a trash bin'[15] so those who are unsure, unwilling, or uninterested have an option that doesn't ruin the efforts of those that recycle.

A clever rubbish addition.

Press for placebo

Adding options can afford a sense of control, and this can be useful for customer-instigated processes, even when it's fake.

There are people who'll tap the side of their nose and tell you that the 'close door' buttons in elevators don't do anything. Unlike most tap-nose people who like a good conspiracy theory, they're correct. Nick Paumgarten of the *New Yorker* explains: 'In most elevators, at least in any built or installed since the early nineties, the door-close button doesn't work. It is there mainly to make you think it works. (It does work if, say, a fireman needs to take control. But you need a key, and a fire, to do that.)'[16]

It's not just elevators that fall prey to the placebo button. Pedestrian crossings are known placebo-button users, from Scotland all the way to New York.

'The city [of New York] deactivated most of the pedestrian buttons long ago with the emergence of computer-controlled traffic signals . . . Any benefit from them [pedestrian buttons] is only imagined', says the *New York Times*.[17] Over 75% of the 3,000+ pedestrian 'walk' buttons in the city function as placebos.

Decoy gear

In the UK, London's Cycle Hire scheme has been in place since July 2010. Bikes are available to rent for a small fee for a length of time and are collected from, and dropped off at, docking stations around the city. Over 100,000 people have signed up and over 2 million journeys have been made. It has been cited as a success.

But not for the right reasons.

By numbers of hires, yes it is a success; but by carbon emissions reductions, no. And that is the statistic by which it should be measured. Transport for London's own study found that 35% of those hiring bikes are tube converts, 29% used to walk, and 23% have switched from bus rides. Only 13% have switched from driving to cycling.[18]

However, the influence of the scheme can be measured in another way – a way that runs counter to the minimum condition of most choice models which state that the introduction of a new alternative *cannot* increase the probability of choosing a member of the original set.[19]

The 'new alternative' is the Cycle Hire bikes, a member of the original set is retail bike shops, and the 'increase in choosing a member of the original set' is being expressed by shops reporting a hike in sales, as reported by the UK Government's Cabinet Office Behavioural Insights Team, and in Bike Europe's Market Report for 2010, which states: 'London's bike shops benefited from the Barclays-sponsored Cycle Hire scheme. It got new people on bikes and the trickle-down effect was to see new people trickling into dealers, enthused about cycling.'[20]

Lipsmackin' thirstquenchin' acetastin' motivatin' goodbuzzin' cooltalkin' highwalkin' fastlivin' evergivin' coolfizzin' Pepsi[21]

Pepsi Cola and Coca-Cola were fighting for market share in the seventies and eighties: Coke was losing. Pepsi introduced a 'taste test' in their 'Pepsi Challenge' TV commercials which showed a simple blind tasting between Pepsi and Coke performed by members of the public in shopping malls. Pepsi came out top primarily because it was sweeter.

Coke freaked.

They introduced New Coke to combat Pepsi Cola's 'taste test' success, and retired the original Coke recipe. It was a poor decision: they could've added New Coke as a third candidate next to the Coca-Cola and Pepsi Cola duo, evoking the 'decoy effect'.

Less than three month later Coke was forced to bring back the original recipe. (It was such an important success for Pepsi they gave their entire staff worldwide a day's holiday.)

11 Take away options

'Simplicity, simplicity, simplicity!'

Henry David Thoreau (1817–62)

I know. I'm sorry. I just spent the previous chapter waxing lyrical about the benefits of 'adding options', and here I am proposing the opposite. Without even a buffer: without an attempt at a soft landing. I switched teams. I'm a turncoat. I'm riddled with inconsistency. It's true. However, I'm only reflecting the way in which we connect with the world. A world that is awash with information, and choice: a few centuries ago a lifetime of knowledge was equivalent to the amount of information contained in tomorrow's broadsheet newspaper. (Although probably less about TV schedules, and the five-day weather forecast.)

In modern times we've built a stable legal system – and a democracy that upholds it – in order to enjoy the freedom and opportunities of which our ancient selves could only dream. This is a good thing. This is a great thing. Except when it's not – just ask the ice hockey federation who eliminated the risk of serious head injury for players without any loss of competitiveness by making helmets compulsory.[1]

This is how you ask with fewer choices to make better outcomes.

Put a lid on it

Switches you flick. Strings you pull. And rubbish you throw in a bin. At least, most people throw rubbish in a bin. And it's been that way for decades. But now we have the demands of recycling, and everything's gone a bit haywire.

In England, the volume of waste that goes to landfill is over 45%. That might sound pretty good until you compare it with Germany, where 1% of waste goes to landfill. In the USA, recycling rates are between 30 and 50% depending on the material (40% of physical space in US landfill is paper according to the EPA). And most of it's done at home: offices lag. There's definitely room for improvement.

Plenty of studies into attitudes to recycling have been done – but of those that display measurable positive attitudes they rarely consider the immediate surroundings. And there have been 'messaging about' and 'proximity to' recycling studies, but they never focused on the shape of the bin. Not one. It was all open-topped bins. Would this make a difference?

Also, recycling bins suffer from the problem of cross-contamination, where landfill and/or food waste is found in recycling bins, which renders all the recycling useless. No one considered testing lids, or lid shape, in reference to this problem.

There were holes in the research: Sean Duffy and Michelle Verges plugged them.

They are, or were at the time, respectively, associate professor of psychology at Rutgers–Camden, and assistant professor at Indiana University, and they studied the effectiveness of recycling bins that have holes shaped to replicate the item to be disposed.[2] Admittedly, shaped lids are not a new invention – I'm sure we've seen examples.

But are they any good?

Duffy and Verges arranged bins side-by-side in groups of three. They were all prominently stickered as either 'Trash', 'Aluminum-Glass-Plastic' or 'Paper'. Some groups-of-three had open lids, replicating standard waste containers. Other groups-of-three had shaped lids: the 'Trash' option had a pushable flap; 'Aluminum-Glass-Plastic' had a pushable flap with a circular hole cut out of the centre mirroring the shape of the expected drinks container; 'Paper' had a lid with two slits. There were two sets of results: the first was amazing.

The shaped bin lids increased correct recycling by 35%.

That is a huge jump – rates of increase in the single digits would be received with excitement. But 35% is great. However, it's overshadowed by the second set of results: if the first were amazing, the second were astounding.

It's important that recycling material is kept free from food waste. If that happens – even if it's only one item of food waste – the entire recycling bin is unusable.

The shaped bin lids reduced food-waste contamination by 95%. Ninety-five per cent.

Why such potent results?

Usually we throw things away while we're doing something else – like using a smart phone, chatting to friends, or thinking about where we're going. A shaped lid creates cognitive load: you have to stop and concentrate on what you're doing. You have to give it your full attention. This is enough to get to our 95% figure.

Throwing things away while doing something else is a very common condition, and one not limited to recycling. For example, while writing this book, I saw a tweeter post a message saying: 'Colleague gave me a letter to mail. I was so preoccupied texting I almost slotted it into the bin next to the postbox.'[3] Multiple demands that compete for our attention have a significant influence on our ability to engage clearly with our surroundings.

But that may not be the effect in its entirety. Duffy and Verges also suggest that shaped lids may be the equivalent of screaming, 'Yo! I'm a recycling bin', which chimes with the pull-out in the previous chapter in which the National University of Singapore are 'pairing every set of recycling bins with a trash bin',[4] so as not to contaminate the recycling. The pairing creates contrast – the 'Yo, I'm a bin . . .' thing.

But, however we get to such stunning results, I think the underlying success is best summed up by Duffy and Verges when they say: 'Placing an object through a small hole or narrow slit requires guided action and cognitive effort not required when simply discarding recyclables into recycling containers having wide openings.'[5]

Remove the option to half-engage with disposing of waste and you get a more competent result. But (yet again) this raises an awkward question: who are we? Are we the people who don't engage with recycling? Or are we the people who do engage with recycling?

The answer to that depends on the shape of the lid.

Less (choice) is more

People never ask for deadlines to be brought forward – never ask for their liberty to be removed. Why would they? Taking away options is oppressive. And anyway is unnecessary for rational actors in a rational world: 'in the rational model, having more time and more options can't make you worse off: more choice does not reduce your welfare',[6] explain Rachel Glennerster and Michael Kremer of the *Boston Review*.

In a rational world, we don't procrastinate. But we don't live in that world – we do procrastinate. The fix? '. . . if you are a procrastinator, you may be better off with a deadline and may prefer to impose a deadline on yourself'.[7]

Dan Ariely of Duke University used three classes of his students to test three different deadline profiles for their end of term papers.[8] One class had one universal deadline at the end of the term for all three papers. Simple, and liberal. No one was unhappy with it.

A second class were told they had three deadlines, one for each of their three papers, but they had a week to decide what they'd be and then commit to them. There was to be a penalty for late submission.

The third and final class were given the 'dictator' treatment: three deadlines, one for each paper, evenly spaced throughout the term, with no compromise, and no discussion.

Which group achieved the highest grades?

In a perfect world the first class with only one universal deadline has the best scenario – you can write at any time, submit in any order, you can rework, switch, take a break, cram it. You have the most liberty because you have the most options. But it wasn't this class that performed the best. In fact, they performed the worst: the classic procrastinator's end-of-term scramble saw them awarded the worst set of grades, both individually and as a group. Second place in terms of group and individual grades went to the second class who had self-imposed deadlines.

It was the dictator group who performed the best, achieving the highest grades in all respects.

And this isn't the only way in which the calibre of intellectual endeavour is improved – counter-intuitively – by the restriction of choice. Sheena Iyengar and Mark Lepper, from Columbia and Stanford Universities respectively, presented a group of students with the task of writing a critical appraisal of a film. The rub? One group was given a choice of six topics from which to choose, the other thirty topics.[9] They didn't know they were being tested, so this was a true measure of their private desires and motivations.

They were asked to choose one topic, and write it up.

Those in the limited choice group outperformed in every area: the number of completed essays was higher, by 74% to 60%, and the grades were higher too. But the really counter-intuitive part is the realization that the same essay topics were in both groups, which means 'that the same choice selected from a limited-choice set can lead to better performance than if the same option had been selected from an extensive-choice set'.[10]

Less choice really *is* more.

So how do we apply this? Topic choice and delivery dates aren't obvious tactics to employ to serve strategies that reduce resource-stress, but as we move towards generating new technology, infrastructure, and communications we will be simultaneously generating and drawing on pools of knowledge and information to achieve the outcomes we need. As opposed to an incontinent approach, clarifying and focusing on defined areas of investigation appears to yield better results, but who knows where to focus attention? And even though that is a difficult question to answer, why not strive to generate work of the highest calibre?

As much as that may seem like a problem for someone else at another time, the contradiction of less choice creating higher-calibre outcomes isn't solely the prerogative of a distant intellectual endeavour – it is a condition that can be ascribed to consumer choice equally well.

For American employees without the relevant vocational financial training (most people), information about retirement plans can get very complicated, very quickly. This affects the decisions made, and they are important because the effects will be felt for years. In one study, participation in retirement plans fell from 75% to fewer than 70% when the number of choices rose from two to fifty-nine. And of those who stuck with the overwhelming number of options and actually made a choice, it was not the best available.[11]

It's hard. 'When we make decisions, we compare bundles of information. So a decision is harder if the amount of information you have to juggle is greater', says Sheena Iyengar in *The Art of Choosing*.[12] Sharon Begley writes in *Newsweek* about the outcomes of choice complexity only affecting us when the stakes are high, but for choices where the stakes are low, like 'For mustard or socks, this may not be a problem'.[13]

Turns out, it is.

The comparative simplicity of products like mustard, or socks – or jam – compared to the complexity of pensions is no guide to people's ability to avoid being overwhelmed by choice.

Introducing again Sheena Iyengar and Mark Lepper, they examined the effects of product range using exotic jams in a grocery store in Menlo Park, California.[14] The store is known for its extensive range of items, so an experiment containing a large number of choices would not look out of place. Rather quaintly, to fit in with the upmarket store, the jams used were manufactured by Wilkin & Sons, who are Purveyors to Her Majesty the Queen. They certainly were desirable.

Two stalls were set up on two different weekends, carrying a number of the jams. For one weekend there were six jams, for the other there were twenty-four.

The outcome?

More people stopped by to taste the range of twenty-four than the range of six. We could've guessed that, I'm sure. It was 60/40 in favour of the larger range. And those who did stop tasted as-near-as-damn-it the same number of jams per person.

But I bet you won't guess the sales figures? One group sold jam to 30% of those who stopped. The other group sold jam to only 3%.

It was the six-jam range that sold the most – in both percentage and absolute numbers.

Why? Sometimes lots of choice can mean no choice at all.

For a start, lots of choice makes us wade through a lot of options to find our preference. And then, if we find our 'preference', it has only a tenuous claim to that title because it requires us to forgo all the others. We don't like to forgo – we have trouble with 'loss'.

However, reducing the number of options means we're more likely to reach a decision, and, when we do, more likely to feel satisfied with our choice because the number of options we *don't* chose – or 'lose' – is small.

Less (information) is more

Argentine farmers rely on accurate seasonal climate forecasts to manage their crops – their livelihood depends upon it – but the real skill is in knowing how to modify decisions in response to forecasts under El Niño or La Niña. It is not a condition many farmers around the world have to contend with. And it takes a lot of effort. Added to that, they have to consider the fluid political situation in Argentina and its effects on taxation. This is over and above their concern about fluctuating prices of crops at harvest, and the cost of fertilizer.

This perfect storm affects decisions in unexpected ways.

James Hansen, Sabine Marx, and Elke Weber authored a study of the Argentine Pampas and South Florida to test how the perceptions and expectations of climate affected farmers' decision making.[15]

Argentine farmers rated their concerns about four areas: the political effects on taxes; weather; cost of purchases; price of sales at harvest. They were asked to rate their concerns on two occasions, where the forecast for La Niña was either favourable or unfavourable.

The spectre of La Niña loomed large when the forecast was unfavourable, so the recorded concern about its effects shot up. This had a rather interesting effect on the concern around political risk and taxes – concern dropped, even though there was no objective change in political risk with or without La Niña. This indicated what the researches called a 'finite pool of worry'.[16] And it is not without consequence – the farmers made different decisions about crops and pricing depending on their answers.

There is an important takeout: legislators need to be very careful not to add to the burden of worry, as do marketers. There's no benefit in shovelling concern at an audience. One needs to be careful to consider a 'portfolio of risk' that is neither too extensive nor too potent. This acknowledges the affective reality without being overwhelming. And this includes references to climate change – its effects have to be dealt with carefully.

We can only deal with so much.

So whether we're talking about information, choice, or the physical world, taking away options can help us to make more precise decisions and create better outcomes. In some cases, it's the only thing that gets us to the party in the first place. As Dan Ariely says, 'simplification is one mark of real genius'.[17]

That's genius.

Help

If you were hurt, or attacked, in a public place I bet you'd want people around you – the more the merrier? More eyes, more ears, more people to help you?

Or so you'd think.

Kitty Genovese was attacked, raped, and murdered, in New York in the spring of 1964. There were thrity-eight witnesses – or so it was reported. It is more likely that few of them saw or heard the attack in its entirety, but they all heard something, and the apparent lack of help given to Kitty shocked the country.

Social psychologists John Darley and Bibb Latané started research into what became known as the 'bystander effect' [18] (to some, the Genovese syndrome), where the larger the number of observers the less likely any will help: everyone thinks someone else will do something.

To reduce the bystander effect you're better off with a small group. Or maybe even only one person – because the burden of responsibility falls on to them.

A head for tragedy

Thomas Shelling, a Californian son of a US naval officer, is a Nobel Prize winning economist and expert in understanding cooperation and conflict[19] – an area of study as applicable to his work in game theory and nuclear arms for the US government as it is for ice hockey.

He noticed that ice hockey players rarely wore helmets even though they risked severe head injury and death, but in secret ballots most players wanted to wear helmets, and many wished it were a requirement.[20]

Why the contradiction?

Not wearing a helmet gave a player an advantage – although pretty small. But once one player took it, others felt they had to. It was a spiral – an arms race. A race that saw them make a collectively poor decision, because if they all wore helmets no one would have an advantage and neither would they have the risk of severe head injury.

The situation was resolved when the authorities made helmets compulsory. And with that, the players' helmet-wearing dilemma was eliminated and they were able to make a collectively better decision.

It is not only ice hockey where we see this effect. Managing our impact on climate change is burdened by situations where individual advantage leads to collectively poorer decisions. Without technological and infrastructural change, the only way to reduce our expression of green house gases today is – unsurprisingly – to reduce the actions that cause it. But this is the 'ice hockey helmet' problem again: if I'm making sacrifices someone else can reap the benefits.

This is where many people – and businesses – want statutory change, even though this desire is rarely expressed publicly.

James Surowiecki writes in the *New Yorker* that around 75% of Americans vote for increases in fuel economy standards if asked. He says: 'We [in the USA] buy gas guzzlers but vote for gas sipping.'[21]

It is a classic 'Tragedy of the Commons' situation,[22] – livestock farmers using common grazing land can introduce extra livestock and reap 100% of the benefits of the sale, while forcing the down sides of over-grazing to be spread equally among the other farmers. This 'arms race' of personal advantage at the expense of the group leads to a collapse in the sustainability of the grazing: all farmers lose the communal grazing, and have no way of feeding their livestock. (Hence, the 'tragedy' bit.)

As Garret Hardin – author of the 'Tragedy of the Commons' paper – is at pains to point out, there is no 'technical solution'[23] to the problem. He asks us to consider a game of tick-tack-toe and how impossible it is to win if you go second unless you abandon the game by bonking your opponent over the head or falsify the records: neither is a 'technical solution'.

There may be behavioural solutions. One possibility is the evocation of the 'reputation effect' in appropriate situations that can help reduce private gain at public expense by making the private gain public. (This is described in more detail in chapter 13, 'Ask using the right *fake* authority', with the experiments of Manfred Milinski, Dirk Semmann, and Hans-Jürgen Krambeck.)

Hardin describes pollution as a Tragedy of the Commons problem 'in reverse', where something is 'put in' rather than 'taken out'. Steven E. Landsburg calls it the 'communal-stream principle' in his book *More Sex Is Safer Sex*: 'Feel free to pollute your own swimming pool, but if your sludge spills over into the stream we all share, you should pay for the damage.'[24]

Is our atmosphere the 'commons', and is our lack of solutions the 'tragedy'? Quite possibly, say Richard H. Thaler and Cass R. Sunstein in the *Chicago Tribune*: 'Climate change could turn out to be the biggest tragedy of the commons in human history.'[25]

12 Ask using the right authority

I confirm I will read this chapter with maximum concentration.

[sign here]_____

Stanley Milgram's famous study of obedience in the 1960s saw 65% of volunteers give what they thought was a fatal electric shock to another human being, despite more than 99% saying they wouldn't.[1] Housed in a prestigious institution, the inability to see the victims, and the physical presence of a lab-coated experimenter delivering instructions, was all the 'authority' they needed.

Enough, in fact, to murder.

Milgram's experiment – despite being effective – is not transposable to any obvious climate change or resource-stress scenarios. And indeed, even if it were, is a little dramatic. However, it does show us how susceptible we are to 'authority' in the broadest sense, and how we perform under observation from those in whom we invest authority – whether that authority is real or imagined. (What is the difference to the observer anyway?)

Authority is always reliant on the messenger and the context in which it's delivered. In the absence of lab-coated technicians instructing us to murder people, how else do we ask using the 'right' authority?

The smell of the greasepaint, the roar of the authority

Celebrity. It's an obvious place to start. People with authority, or influence, are usually celebrities. But they don't have to be in entertainment – business sectors have famous participants. They can even be politicians, like the President of the USA.

Obama visited a Home Depot store as part of a retro-fitting drive and said, 'I know the idea [of investing in upgrades to inefficient buildings] may not be very glamorous, although I get really excited about it. Insulation is sexy stuff.'[2] Insulation as 'sexy' is some claim.

Obama has also visited Opower in Arlington, a company which uses persuasion techniques pioneered by Robert Cialdini and his team to reduce energy consumption in homes across California. The UK Prime Minister, David Cameron, said of their work in a Behavioural Economics presentation at a global conference called TED, 'Behavioural Economics can transform people's behaviour in a way that all the bullying and badgering from a Government cannot possibly achieve.'[3]

This kind of endorsement is powerful, and all well and good if you have access to this authority 'solution', but few have access to current heads of government. So who else can create authoritative messaging – the legislature? They do have authority, but mostly in terms of describing what we can't do, and that sort of legislation needs policing which can be expensive, and it often uses up social capital (makes people feel their actions are being curtailed). It's difficult for legislation to be elegant.

The 'Don't Mess with Texas' 1980s American littering campaign had authority, but wasn't successful because of legislation or policing. It is a very famous campaign that has been written up extensively and well, including in Chip and Dan Heath's book *Made to Stick*.[4] In the 1980s Texan youth would not stop littering on the highways, despite fines in the thousands of dollars: the law was not authority enough. But Texas's sporting and country-music heroes were people the youth aspired to be, and impress: they had authority. A commercial television campaign was created and filmed using home-grown stars such as Lance Armstrong, Chuck Norris, Willie Nelson, Lyle Lovett, Owen Wilson, and others, who all spoke directly to camera imploring the viewer to stop 'messing with Texas', as they were shown throwing litter in a bin. The use of respected celebrities cleverly avoided negatives of guilt and shame that legislation leans on by focusing on the positives of pride and group identity.

Within five years roadside litter was down by over 70%.

The 'respected celebrity' as voice-piece is starting to happen of its own accord on social media – particularly on Twitter – and with comments directly related to sustainable solutions. Robert Llewellyn, originally a stand-up comedian, most famously Krighton from a TV series called *Red Dwarf*, and now a TV presenter, is a self-confessed electric car nut. After a journey in one of his cars, he tweets: 'Back home after mammoth electric car day. 104 miles in electric car, re-charge in the middle, tiddly poodly doo'.[5] And Edward Norton – the Hollywood film-maker and actor in *American History X* and *Fight Club* tweets: 'Had a Prius Plug-In for a week test. Fully electric for short trips, then hybrid kicks in when you need it. Very efficient. Silent. Cool.'[6]

It may seem benign, but their authority is made all the more potent by being tweeted to people who actively choose to follow them. It's a self-selecting version of 'Don't Mess With Texas'.

These are positive solutions to resource-stress from media figures. The media business and reporting as a whole have authority, but have shown an inconsistent relationship between the needs of balanced reporting and scientific discourse. This is a challenge to its relevance, despite its obvious authority.

Maxwell Boykoff from Oxford University wrote a paper called 'Flogging a dead norm?'[7] in which he examined newspaper coverage of climate change in the USA and the UK during the mid-2000s. He found that while scientific consensus stated that climate change was human-influenced, reporting in the USA (unlike in the UK) presented anthropogenic and non-anthropogenic arguments in a proportion that didn't represent the science. Journalists were reporting a two-sided debate that didn't really exist – by the end of that decade 97% of climate scientists agreed human activity contributed to climate change.[8]

This has had a measurable effect on attitudes. A review of surveys on public attitudes to climate change shows around 10–15% do not believe human activities are the cause, but over 50% agree that 'many leading experts still question if human activity is contributing to climate change'.[9] For the record, the USA and the UK appear to be more 'hawk'-like than Europe.

Is there a solution? Putting science and scientists front-and-centre isn't always the answer, even though they are the ones with the answers.

The problem is that there's scientific uncertainty with the dates and severity of climate change effects. This is terrifically effective at undermining authority – not because the system is complex but because of how we understand complexity. The human mind likes simple, local, immediate, and linear situations that have some certainty and are easy to 'bring to life'. Climate change is almost the opposite – complex, global, delayed, and with non-linear effects of carbon outputs, the total picture creates uncertainty. It's a surprise as a species we're even talking about it, when viewed through this prism.

This four-dimensional modelling of our understanding of the world is thanks to work on the Construal-Level Theory from Trope and Liberman.[10] As an antidote to the prevalence and potency of uncertainty around climate effects, Shackley and Wynne have defined 'boundary-ordering devices' that minimize the problems. These involve 'quantification' and 'locating uncertainty', which helps to make concrete as much of known information as possible. Also, scheduling reductions in uncertainty on expectation of more precise data creates a future that increases in certainty at known intervals.[11] These all make the problems more tractable. (These categories sound a little like Donald Rumsfeld's 'known-knowns', 'known-unknowns', 'unknown-unknowns', post-Iraq invasion speech.[12])

More tractable definitions help in selling future products too. BBC Radio 4's midday topical discussion show *You & Yours* featured a piece on aviation biofuels during which they interviewed Paul Steele, the Executive Director of the Air Transport Action Group, which is a worldwide alliance of businesses promoting economically beneficial aviation. He was talking about advances in algae fuels, which are way ahead of expectation in terms of volume of production and use.[13] But he was unable to deliver any concrete sense of what future growth might look like – not through want of enthusiasm or desire – because his explanation played into Construal-Level Theory's soft future dimensions: some time in the future, by someone else, somewhere else, for the benefit of someone else. We often summarize information such as this as a 'remote possibility' even when the outcome is highly probable if the 'when', 'who', 'where', and 'for whom' are unclear. Boundary-ordering devices would've helped Paul Steele tremendously: 'quantification', 'locating uncertainty', and scheduling when uncertainty can be reduced through the collection of more precise data.

Understanding our perceptual quirks can help us to look back as well as forward with clarity.

You can have any colour you like, as long as it's authority

Private and shareholder-owned brands, and the businesses they represent, are increasingly embedded in the fabric of society, and as such are important authority figures. 'If taking action on climate change is seen as an economic issue, it may be most credibly conveyed by a business person who has done it.'[14]

Ray Anderson is an authority for business. He founded Interface, Inc., which makes carpet tiling, and can genuinely claim to be a 'business person who has done it': Interface, Inc. cut total carbon dioxide emissions by over 60%, and has made 111 million square yards of climate-neutral carpet since 2003. It has been named several times by *Fortune* magazine as one of the '100 Best Companies to Work For'. He is recognized all over the world and speaks regularly on turning his petroleum-heavy carpet business into one of the most sustainable on the planet. He says: 'If we can do it, anybody can. If anybody can, everybody can.'[15]

Similarly, brands and businesses can act as an authority for consumers – something not lost on Daniel Ratchford from Sutton Council in the UK. They wanted to make 6,000 rolls of loft insulation available at massively reduced prices to residents of Sutton. It makes sense because it's 'a very simple step to make their homes more carbon efficient and to save on their bills', says Daniel.[16] The masterstroke was collaborating with the UK's largest home improvement business, B&Q, to store and sell the insulation. As a well-known and trusted business, they 'wash' the campaign in authority, and normality.

It's not only a case of recognizing that businesses and brands lend authority – some are demanding they do it. Investors and shareholders increasingly want business strategy explained in a carbon-constrained or resource-stressed world (some investors and shareholders are even 'asking' for this explanation in the form of a lawsuit).[17] Many businesses are responding to this request to prove leadership and planning with actions as well as information.

Apple pulled out of the US Chamber of Commerce (USCC) and Nike resigned from the board after the USCC made increasingly erratic comments about carbon and climate change, with one board member calling for a

'Scopes *Monkey Trial*'[18] on climate change.[19] Similarly, IBM sponsored four reports written by a company called Acclimatise, who specialize in risk management, to use their expertise to deal with climate risks. One of the four reports is written for oil and gas companies exploring the implications of climate change on their businesses.[20] They've identified the direct and indirect effects on infrastructure and equipment of sea-level rises (raising assets higher, moving or building further inland)[21] amongst other effects, but one of the most interesting challenges is the Alaska pipeline. It was engineered for permafrost conditions based on temperature records between 1950 and 1970, which happened to be the coldest two decades on record. As the climate warms and the permafrost softens, the pipeline is reaching the limits of its design, and the limits of its operation.[22]

IBM, the oil companies, Apple, and Nike? That's quite some authority.

Moser and Dilling say in their paper about communicating climate change: 'Trust in the messenger is particularly important in the context of a problem like climate change that is invisible, uncertain, seemingly remote in time and space, scientifically and morally complex.'[23] They explain the authority of the messenger as able to calm the effects of almost the exact same dimensions that Trope and Liberman identify as problematic in their Construal-Level Theory (here/not here, now/not now, me/not me, clear/ unclear). You could also say the right authority acts as a pseudo Shackley and Wynne 'boundary-ordering device' in that quantification of the problem, locating uncertainties, and scheduled assessment of risk are all implied in a business's desire to keep trading in the future.

Trust in the messenger is certainly important. And in the form of big business and the challenges of dealing with climate change, to be effective beyond the boardroom and the AGM it must be 'overt'. But the 'overt–obvious' complex doesn't sufficiently scribe the boundary of authoritative communication.

The area is larger.

Those who have authority thrust upon them

Parents, usually, are authority figures. But instead of 'authority figures', how about defining them as 'figures that have authority'? It's a subtle distinction, but one that allows other members of a family to become the 'right authority' to ask a question.

In *The Tipping Point*,[24] Malcolm Gladwell describes how the percentage of adults wearing seatbelts in 1960s USA languished in the low teens. For years the US government attempted to force drivers and passengers to wear their safety belts. Fines were instituted in many states, but drivers resented this – America is the Land of the Free and the Home of the Brave, after all, and if a driver was feeling brave and wanted to be free of a safety belt, then that's exactly what they'd do. This tendril of legislation creeping into private space was un-American. The battle lines were drawn, and remained strong, until one tweak to the legislation. Its effects were a surprise to everyone.

Child seatbelt laws were passed.

It was fairly simple – children who didn't need baby seats or boosters were required to wear seatbelts while travelling in the rear of a car. Gladwell asserts that from this point onwards, children wearing seat belts – quite innocently – asked their parents why they weren't wearing theirs. All of a sudden, an act of liberation and defiance was cast as an act of familial hypocrisy. As Consumerology write, our biology sets off alarm bells by making us 'feel bad because widespread hypocrisy is a drag on the survival of the group'.[25]

Seatbelt use in America today is above 70%.

More anecdotally, but an equally clear picture of children-as-authority (although an authority opposing anthropogenic climate change), a tweeter told me about the challenges of creating a 'Tropical island' style children's party that included turning the house temperature up: 'On top of if all, children are being sanctimonious at me about failing to "sauve le planète"!': familial hypocrisy compounding the stress of party preparation.

Keep your friends close, and your authority closer

'Signature shot', 'signature move', and 'signature tune': signatures are part of who we are. And while we may not all have a 'signature move' (except that man from the Accounts Department who has a few too many complimentary drinks every Christmas and 'dances'), we all have a handwritten signature – the one that goes on credit cards, package collection forms, purchase agreements, driving licences, and purchases (except in areas where PIN cards are used) amongst other things – so what?

Your signature influences your behaviour.

It's as simple as that – the mere act of signing affects your subsequent behaviour.[26] It doesn't matter what your signature is, only that you inscribe it.

Keri Kettle and Gerald Häubl from the University of Alberta's Business School are the first people to demonstrate what they call this 'signature effect'. They say it acts as a self-identity prime,[27] which has interesting effects for consumers and retailers alike. They give us a 'for-instance', postulating that a recreational runner who has 'just purchased groceries using her credit card [in countries where they require a signature] is probably not aware that signing the credit card slip is causing her to now spend more time shopping in the sporting goods store next door'.[28]

The self-identity prime gets us fervently to approve choice that matches our self-identity *and* to dismiss less relevant choice with equal passion. Our ferocity towards identity approvals is compounded by a quicker response, too (they timed people with a stopwatch in a supermarket experiment).

But you must let signatures breathe, as 'disrupted' signing doesn't seem to work very well – such as on digital signature pads common to delivery services, or in small awkward spaces that affect the hand.[29] In fact Richie Zweigenhaft's research on signature size linked it to self-esteem: the bigger the better in that regard.[30]

It certainly creates interesting marketing opportunities, and one must wonder about the unintended effects of supermarket/shop prize draws or research questions that require a signature.

Interestingly, Steve Martin, co-author of *Yes! 50 Scientifically Proven Ways to Be Persuasive*, points out that in a court of law you're required to give a verbal oath before giving verbal evidence, but only required to give a signature of declaration at the end of a written testimony. This ordering surely must affect outcomes if the signature effect is so strong? Would the quality of information given on insurance and application forms increase if the self-identity prime was evoked by requiring a signature at the beginning of the form instead of at the end?[31] As is common with the issues of choice architecture, once one understands that context denies neutral presentation, one sees it everywhere. (Even in court, Your Honour.)

(You noticed I put a joke confirmation signature at the beginning of this chapter to evoke the self-identity prime. I doubt anyone will sign it. Did you?)

It takes very little imagination to port this effect straight across into any sustainable initiative that could benefit from binding people into a sense of ownership. I'm sure UK village shopkeeper Yvonne Froud and the 'suits' at Bud Light in the USA haven't read the signature research, but they're nipping at its heels with some rather inventive ideas.

Yvonne has all but stopped children littering in her village by marking sweet wrappers with the names of those who buy them.[32] It would be interesting to see the effects of children self-signing sweet wrappers. And Bud Light in the US have a new bottle with a signature panel pre-printed for customers to write a name, a phone number, a joke – anything to personalize it. Interesting toes-in-the-water, and perhaps something a UK bank could've learned from when they sent their customer, Chris Lancaster from Essex, a bank card bearing the name 'Mr C Lancaster Dick Head'.[33]

They have since apologized. (And he never used it.)

Despite Chris's unfortunate incident, 'authority' is found in a variety of obvious (and not so obvious) people and places that are just as effective and much more practical than Stanley Milgram's electric shock killing lab.

No lab-coat required.

13 Ask using the right *fake* authority

'Here's looking at you, kid.'

Rick Blaine, *Casablanca* (1942)

Kismet is a robot.[1] It belongs to the Massachusetts Institute of Technology and is designed to mimic the facial expressions of humans. It has eyes, eyebrows, ears, and a mouth. They move, too. But there is no disguising the fact that it looks like a hardware store sculpture that's waiting for a prosthetic face; no one would confuse it with a human (even for a split second). However, despite this, Kismet can evoke deep-seated responses in humans.

Even a simple photo of Kismet is powerful enough, as Terry Burnham and Brian Hare from Harvard discovered half a decade ago.

They investigated charitable donation – a puzzle for Darwinian evolution because it levies a cost without a benefit – by testing the effects of reputation on participants. Nearly one hundred volunteers played a donation game where they were told a communal pot would deliver maximum yield as long as others donated too.[2] All of them chose their donation amount at a computer, alone. Half of the computers contained a photo of Kismet's face. (Just a photo.)

The volunteers who had the cute robot in their eye-line while making a decision donated 30% more than the others. Why?

Rationally, you and I know that a 'hardware store' sculpture of a human face is a poor facsimile at best but, as Burham says, we get fooled by 'a pair of fake eyeballs because ancient parts of our brain fail to recognise them as fake.'[3] We act as if we're being watched. And because we're evolutionarily familiar with living in small groups, being watched affects our reputation – being seen to be generous might mean increased chance of future gifts or decreased chance of future punishment.

All this from a fake pair of eyeballs, in a photograph, that remained unmentioned.

Authority doesn't get any more 'fake' than that.

Real vision

A few years ago Melissa Bateson, Daniel Nettle, and Gilbert Roberts of the psychology department of Newcastle University, UK, made a small tweak to their tea and coffee 'honesty box'[4] (a box for collecting small voluntary payments for the use of tea, coffee, and accoutrements). None of their co-workers knew of the experiment, or noticed it.

Even so, the small tweak drastically changed the department's behaviour.

The 'honour' payment system had been in place for years. Money was collected in a small box on the kitchen counter-top. There was a small A5-size sign taped at eye-level to a cupboard indicating suggested prices for each commodity: thirty pence for tea, fifty pence for coffee, ten pence for the use of milk. Even though they were far too inexpensive to cause anyone financial hardship, the layout of the room meant that anyone who wanted to skip payment could do so without being observed.

Over ten weeks, Melissa and the team appended a letterbox-shaped image to the price sheet. They alternated weekly between a horizontal image of flowers, and a horizontal close-up photograph of a human face filling the strip. They were images of men and women of different ages, but always had their eyes looking directly at the viewer.

The team measured milk consumption and used it as a proxy for the total amount of tea and coffee consumed by dividing the monies raised by milk consumed. In this way, they could measure the effect of the different images. And it was rather odd.

Contributions always increased in the weeks when the eyes were displayed, and decreased when the flowers were shown.

But it was the size of the effect that was staggering: Staff paid well over 250% more for their drinks than they did in the other weeks. 'Frankly we were staggered by the size of the effect',[5] Roberts told *New Scientist* magazine.

As am I, especially as it was 'in a real-world context where participants were . . . using their own money'.[6]

They ascribe the stunningly large effect of the image of the eyes to inducing a perception of being watched. This is important because the act of being watched stores information in social groups in the form of reputation. And the self-interested motive of reputation maintenance may be sufficient to explain co-operation in the absence of direct return. This is particularly relevant in large groups where first-hand knowledge is missing because potential co-operating partners can only act on knowledge about each other's reputation.[7] It's a lot like eBay and it's ranking. In fact most digital social networks have some element of a reputation trace provided by a hard-to-fake footprint.

Manfred Milinski, Dirk Semmann, and Hans-Jürgen Krambeck from the Max Planck Institute in Germany looked at how reputation effect can help solve 'Tragedy of the Commons' type problems by setting up two games that could sustain a public resource if played in a particular way.[8]

The first was a simultaneous contribution game for six people (they were strangers, so the group was synthetic). They could contribute a fixed sum of money, or not. Irrespective of who contributed, the total would be doubled and split evenly between them. To maximize the *total* payout, each player should pay in (the payout equalling the sum of six contributions doubled). To maximize an *individual* payout, each player should pay-in except the individual in question who will enjoy one-sixth of the sum of five contributions doubled for zero input. It was in each player's interest to be the individual who received the maximum payout, but without clear agreement to do so, the game soon degenerates into a series of tit-for-tat contribution withholding, reducing the *total* payout and leaving everyone worse off.

However, the second game contained an element of reputation management by introducing a public element. Two players were picked from the group. Each was assigned donor or receiver status. If the donor gave a specified sum of money the receiver would get double – the same mechanism as before. However, this time the donor's decision was displayed on a screen for the rest of the (non-playing) group to see. This act of being observed by the rest of the group affected the reputation of the donor, even within this 'synthetic' group. This was enough to keep the game buoyant, positive, and with a rate of donation agreement at about 65%.

'Tragedy of the Commons' type problems make direct comment on our ability to manage our draw on the communal resource that is our atmosphere and other natural resources. But apart from showing this with tea, coffee, and games – where else can we find significant uses of fake authority?

Smile, you're on camera

In the UK, South Lanarkshire Council has speed signs that respond to the cars as they approach.[9] They are called Vehicle Activated Signs (VAS). They are the size of a flat suitcase and attach to existing street furniture, like lampposts. They are self-contained, and have no data-capture other than forward-facing radar to detect speed. Their LED-type display shows the road's speed limit by default. When a car approaches it switches the display to the oncoming car's speed with the line 'your speed' underneath.

This is not particularly uncommon in the UK, or other countries. What is uncommon is what the sign does next: it shows a very simple 'face' constructed from a circle, with dots for eyes, and a line in place of the mouth that either curves up or down. The oncoming driver sees a 'smiley face' if he is under the speed limit, or a 'sad face' if he is over it. With no fines, and no captured identifiable information, ignoring it has no cost.

And yet, people don't – so much so that speeding has plummeted by over 50% where these signs are used.

Not only is speeding reduced, but average car speeds are also lower in these areas, by up to 14%. Councillor Michael McCann, the then deputy leader of

South Lanarkshire Council, is heartened by this, saying: 'When you consider that a 1mph drop in speed equates to a 5% reduction in accidents, then it's clear that these signs are already having a positive impact on road safety.'[10]

It seems the raw 'behaviour' of the smileys/saddos is plugging straight into our brains without having to negotiate the cognitive layer. We make an intuitive, rapid, and associative effort that evokes the self-interested motive of reputation maintenance and quite possibly our chance of survival – sad faces mean ostracisation and abandonment.

Such a dramatic reduction in speeding is all the more impressive when cast against our certain knowledge that driving is an area of life we're very poor at judging. For instance, only 50% of drivers can be better than average; yet many more of us think we are (in one study into illusory superiority more than 90% of Americans considered themselves better than average).[11] Even when we get direct evidence to the contrary, we rarely adjust our opinion, as Caroline Preston and Stanley Harris discovered in their study of the psychology of drivers who had been in traffic accidents (from 1965),[12] about which Dan Lovallo and Olivier Sibony, writing for the *McKinsey Quarterly*, paraphrase: 'drivers laid up in hospitals for traffic accidents they themselves caused overestimate their driving abilities just as much as the rest of us do'.[13]

Electrifying smiles

On Friday 5 March 2010, President Obama walked onto a podium prepared for him at a small company in Arlington, Virginia and told them that they were an American success story and 'a model of what we want to be seeing all across the country'.[14] That business in Arlington is, according to the *Washington Post*, the 'best example of climate psychology in action'.[15] And they're called Opower.

They owe their origin to a famous experiment by Cialdini, along with Schultz, Nolan, Goldstein, and Griskevicius, called 'The Constructive, Destructive, and Reconstructive Power of Social Norms'.[16] In it they discovered that providing the residents of a street with information about how their energy consumption compared to their neighbours' energy consumption dramatically altered behaviour: those with a higher than average consumption reduced it, and those with lower than average increased it. All Cialdini and his colleagues did was describe the provincial norm.

However, this only resulted in a 'rush to the middle', which failed to change overall energy consumption. A tangible benefit would only be delivered by encouraging the low users to stay low, at the same time as encouraging the high users to modify. This was challenging.

The solution was to present the 'descriptive normative' electricity usage information with an injunctive message of approval to the low users and an injunctive message of disapproval to the high users. But what form did these messages take?

A 'smiley face' for approval; a 'sad face' for disapproval.

In practice, each household electricity bill came with a bar graph showing the highest consumer on the street, the lowest consumer, and the recipient's consumption with the addition of either a 'smiley face' or a 'sad face' depending on usage. This stopped the low users backsliding and encouraged the high users to drop.

And in experimental conditions, it reduced overall electricity consumption by a whopping 40%.

That's a big number. And it pricked the ears of many, including some entrepreneurs who incorporated Opower and built the company around the experiment – on the board of which Cialdini sits. Today they work with power companies all over California using the principles of the experiment and have created immediate and persistent consumption drops of between 1.5% and 3.5% in the field.[17] A drop of this size is a good start in managing resource-stress, particularly as it's immediate, persistent, and consistent without any change to today's technology and infrastructure.

However, there have been some tweaks to the information presentation since the experiment. They use one or two smiley faces now for the low users, and have dispensed with the sad face for the high users, replacing it with the phrase 'Room to improve' and stressing that lower consumption means lower bills as well as helping the environment. It's working. President Obama endorses the work: 'I want companies like OPOWER to be expanding and thriving all across America. It's good for consumers. It's good for our economy It's good for our environment.'[18]

But perhaps there could be more tweaks. Dora Costa and Matthew Kahn are economists from the University of California, Los Angeles. They've dug a little deeper into the responses to the Opower charts and have found different responses based on political affiliation, as reported by Ray Fisman in *Slate* magazine. [19] The overall average electricity consumption drop of about 2% is helped by a 6% drop from previously high-using Liberal voters, is hindered by some core Republican voters who increase consumption by 1% as a response to the information, and is nudged down by a few core Democrats who drop electricity consumption by 3%.

This smiley-descriptive-normative-injunctive device also seems to ameliorate the effects of the Jevons Paradox.

William Stanley Jevons, wrote *The Coal Question: An Enquiry concerning the Progress of the Nation, and the Probable Exhaustion of our Coal-Mines* in 1865, in which he proposed that the more efficient factories became, the more factories there would be, and the greater pressure there would be on coal consumption, eventually leading to its exhaustion.[20]

That didn't quite happen because of efficiencies in coal extraction and a reduction in demand, but the bare bones of the paradox – that greater efficiency puts upward pressure on consumption – is entirely relevant to carbon dioxide emissions today. However, Cialdini *et al.*'s experiment – and indeed Opower itself – seems to have stymied the Jevons paradox by using the fake 'smileys' to evoke the self-interested reputation maintenance motive.

However odd it seems that we adjust our behaviour so fundamentally when confronted with poor facsimiles of our wonderfully expressive faces, or that we value our social capital so much that even a hint of public observance bends our will, Vanessa Woods writing in the *New Scientist* quotes evolutionary anthropologist Daniel Fessler who explains it succinctly: 'Our mental architecture is just not used to the modern environment.'[21]

And that's the reality that underpins our response to fakery.

Part IV

The conversations

Questions that create associations, and associations that create change

Conversari (to associate with) and *convertere* (frequentative; to turn around) are at the root of the questions in 'The conversations'. Sections on feedback, public expression, and issues of ownership show how questions – asked with varying degrees of frequency – can establish potent associations.

Popeye's Chicken & Biscuits on West Cermak Road in Chicago points us in the direction of some light-bulbs, a misinterpreted correlation, and a man named Thomas Edison. That, along with why you hear your name called out in a crowded room, helps us manage energy consumption. Why? Because feedback can find us, and affect us, in many ways.

Knowledge of Semmelweiss's killer cadaverous particles from 1839 was not enough to create the life-saving behaviour that public feedback created 160 years later. And there's no reason why America shouldn't be called the Land of the Free, the Home of the Ranked after the questions that uncovered 'startling' information created positive change without any legislation.

All this, as well as the allocation of rights, killing of pine trees, electricity supplies, coffee mugs, chimpanzees' tea parties and a New York restaurant food tasting are all examples of questions that crystallize ownership in a way that affects behaviour.

'Enjoy the conversations', I say.

14 Let the feedback ask the question

'Everything that can be invented has been invented.'
Charles H. Duell, Commissioner, U.S. Office of Patents, 1899

Popeye's Chicken & Biscuits serves New Orleans style short-order food on the corner of West Cermak Road and South Cicero Avenue in Chicago, about ten miles inland from Lake Michigan. It's a single-storey purpose-built fast-food franchise with a garish sign, plenty of parking, and welcoming staff. It marks one corner of the Hawthorne Shopping Center – a collection of separate shops and a cinema complex common to many shopping centers built in the less expensive industrial areas of US cities. Few visitors know of its importance to the social sciences.

In November 1924, a young man named Walter Shewhart turned off West Cermak Road onto the site of the Hawthorne Shopping Center, but unlike the visitors of today he wasn't looking for Popeye's Chicken & Biscuits.

It wasn't there.

The entire site was a Western Electric factory employing 40,000 men. It was one of the largest manufacturing plants in America.

Walter was a representative of the Committee on the Relation of Quality and Quantity of Illumination to Efficiency – a committee set up to investigate reports by several companies that better lighting in factories increased workers' productivity. Thomas Edison – the chair of the parent committee – invited Western Electric to carry out experiments to demonstrate this relationship. The original aim was to test claims that brighter lighting increased output.

Walter began his tests.[1]

He took some of the workers and spilt them into two: a test team and a control team. His first study found no relationship between lighting and productivity. Continuing, he found that both increases and decreases in lighting increased output. This was not supposed to happen. Confused, he found that changing light bulbs in front of workers increased output, even when the new light bulbs were the same as the old.

This is broadly what we know from the descriptions of the Western Electric Hawthorne factory experiments. Christened the 'Hawthorne Effect' in the 1950s by Henry A. Landsberger,[2] they tell us that by simply being in a trial, performance is altered.

The Hawthorne experiments have since been conflated into the standard bearer for placebo[3] and feedback effects. This may afford the tests greater significance than they deserve, as the results were not properly peer-reviewed and the sample sizes were small, but they do describe a quirk common to us all: 'We pay attention to what we . . . measure.'[4]

Sometimes, the keenest way to ask for change is to let the feedback do the talking.

Glowing recommendation

Making the intangible tangible is quite some trick. A simple version is the light bulb – it makes tangible the flow of electricity. Turn it on and electricity is drawn, and there is light. Turn it off, and there is no electricity drawn, and no light. But rig it in a slightly different way, and you can both measure and present some very interesting intangibles.

Ambient Devices, Inc. is a small company in Cambridge, Massachusetts that manufactures the Ambient Orb and Ambient Beacon. They are made of frosted glass. The Orb is the size and shape of a small football. The Beacon is a square version, the size of half a bottle of wine. They are connected wirelessly to a local phone network and can be programmed to pick up data varying from stock prices and traffic congestion to pollen counts and wind speed. They show changes in the data by glowing different colours.

This might seem a little simple, but it is based on the fundamental insight that we engage with the world through the unconscious accumulation of information called 'pre-attentive processing'. As Ambient Devices, Inc. put it, 'How often have you been in an airport or crowded party and heard your name called out of the acoustic clutter?'[5] (Interestingly, pre-attentive processing is faulty in disorders such as schizophrenia, Alzheimer's disease, and autism.)[6]

David Lewis – a psychologist who advises aircraft-makers on cockpit design, in conversation with *The Economist* – says 'filtering information in this way makes sense . . . since trying to process too much information is a source of stress and can lead to mistakes'.[7]

In the early 2000s some of Ambient Devices, Inc.'s first customers hacked the product to suit their own needs: one couple used the Ambient Orb to track their fertility, and another customer tracked energy-use in his Manhattan apartment relative to other, similar apartments. And it was this energy measurement method that Mark Martinez of Southern California Edison saw as a solution to get his customers to conserve energy.

Electricity generation is tricky because there's no way to store it and it's difficult to increase generation quickly. It's a world of forecasting and guesswork that would be more efficient if power use were consistent. A common incentive to stimulate or retard demand is pricing: higher price when demand is strong and lower when weak – cheap nighttime pricing is one example. Mark Martinez tried to stimulate response by firing off alerts about the cost of electricity via email, automatic phone calls, and text messages to his customers.

None of it changed behaviour. He needed another approach.

He programmed an Ambient Orb to glow turquoise during off-peak hours and red when the price of electricity was at its peak. He bought a hundred or so, and handed them out to the same customers he'd been emailing, texting, and calling.

A few weeks later, peak hour use was down by 40%.[8]

Martinez describes the Orb as having 'a relatively benign effect. But when you suddenly see your ball flashing red, you notice.'[9] He's correct – this ambient information was delivered pre-attentively and timely, thereby avoiding the need for continual foreground cognitive loading. His previous communication via emails, automatic phone calls, and text messages were a toxic combination of 'Push' and 'Pull' information which, even if they were timely, required cognitive effort to engage.

The Ambient Orb in the Martinez configuration is 'on your side'. It is helping you reduce your bills by telling you when prices are high while engaging the minimum cognitive load. However, the immediacy of the intangible made tangible is powerful, and initially can be overwhelming, as this sequence from social media shows:[10]

Scotland

Jan. 2011:	*'Bloke has just arrived to install a new Smart electricity meter. My mind is working overtime. How smart? . .'*[11]
10 mins. later:	*'Now have device with big flashing green light telling me how much electricity and gas I am using, to the penny, every second of the day.'*[12]
13 mins. later:	*'Traumatised. It goes to amber when you switch your kettle on.'*[13]
14 mins. later:	*'I am now actually talking to it when I walk past. "I'm sorry. I was just checking my emails. I've turned it off . . . " It is my new mother.'*[14]
16 mins. later:	*'Am beating myself up already.'*[15]

A device similar to the Ambient Orb is the Waterpebble, designed by Paul Priestman to provide feedback for water use. It's a small oval device that sits in the shower tray and measures water consumed, expressing the amount by changing colour. The inspiration for this was born of his frustration with hotel signs that say 'Please use water sparingly' because they mean very little without quantification.

Ambient feedback that takes advantage of pre-attentive processing is not the only way to generate meaningful feedback. Context can help create meaning, even if it does require a heavier cognitive load. For instance, direct displays on portable electricity use monitors are invariably number based, which gives high-fidelity information in the moment, but rarely any overall context. In 1989 van Houwelingen and van Raaij contextualized one of these portable displays by adding the previous day's energy consumption in relation to a weather-adjusted target.[16] They saw electricity use reduced by 10%, which is pretty consistent with this class of direct feedback methods that typically returning savings in the 5% to 15% region.

Billing data can provide context too, especially as untangling the single charge for energy consumed at different times by different devices has powerful effects. A thousand Norwegian homes understood their usage better with billing in the form of a pie-chart showing a breakdown of households' appliances.[17] And disaggregated billing can show how load is spread over the year – a contextual reference we are usually divorced from – which can help prompt investment by showing the financial effects. This class of 'informative billing' has shown savings of 0% to 12%.[18]

A three-year trial of informative billing in Oslo saw participants change their daily routines so comprehensively that none of them could recall the changes they made unless prompted. An 'informative billing' feedback mechanism like this tends to need about three months to affect permanent change.[19]

Despite all this knowledge and research, many of us still have energy consumption presented as raw numbers arranged in arrears. In 1994 Kempton and Layne drew this analogy: 'consider groceries in a hypothetical store totally without price markings, billed via a monthly statement . . . How could grocery shoppers economise under such a billing regime?'[20]

Not only does one need feedback, but it must be the right type.

('There's been a leak of electricity in aisle 4. A cleaner to aisle 4 please.')

Driving change

Deep-sea fishing and coal mining are the developed world's top two most deadly professions. The third? Driving. A new company called GreenRoad has found a way to make it safer. With backing from Richard Branson and Al Gore amongst others, the core of their offering is a simple dashboard-mounted device the size of a matchbox containing three lights – one green, one yellow, and one red. [21]

It seems laughably simple.

It monitors driving characteristics like braking and swerving. If driving gets more erratic the yellow lights turn on, then the red. GreenRoad drivers crash 50% less than normal. That's good for everyone, including the driver. But one of the consequence of safer driving is lower fuel bills to the tune of 10%.

Immediate feedback is not only the province of commercial drivers.

'Competitive Dad' syndrome is evident in the self-styled 'hypermilers' around the world. A group of Toyota hybrid drivers in the USA compete with each other on fuel economy using the Prius's on-the-fly calculation of fuel consumption. Tom Igoe of New York University says, 'For a long time we have known that people will change their habits if they are exposed to feedback in real time.'[22]

Lee Peterson is an Ohio retail consultant. He used to drive a Jeep before he got a hybrid. He quickly became obsessed with his mileage because of the immediate feedback on the dashboard. One thing he hadn't realized was the effect of hills on fuel use. He says it's only knowledge but 'Now I have it. Knowledge is king.'[23]

However, Sebastian Deterding, a researcher at Hans Bredow Institute for Media Research, writes of the unintended consequences of automotive efficiency feedback. BMW tested a real-world fuel efficiency game using the onboard navigation system – each player tried to use the least amount of fuel over the same route.[24] They were recording average savings of about 1 litre over 250 kilometres, but some were running through traffic lights because stopping and starting penalized efficiency. It seems the competition was not a life and death matter, but more important than that. And feedback was the catalyst.

Oops.

Extending feedback from driving into all areas of transport is a problem Andreas Zachariah solved when faced with the frustration of trying to work out his carbon dioxide impact across multiple journeys and multiple forms of transport. He created a mobile app that uses GPS to record journeys. Its algorithms 'guess' the form of transport by measuring movement – a train will be consistent, fast, and straight, whereas walking will be slower and more nimble. In conversation with Alok Jha for the *Guardian* newspaper the designers say that users can 'easily track their environmental impact and, if they choose, modify their behaviour to lower-carbon alternatives'.[25]

Information alone is not enough to change behaviour, but adding a feedback loop gives that information some context – whether it's a peer-comparison, a timely delivery, or a comparison over time.

Feedback really can be the voice, the words, and the grammar of a 'question' that asks for behaviour change.

Valuable feedback

LinkedIn is a social networking site for business worth billions of dollars. It's free to set up a profile and connect to colleagues and business acquaintances. The real value of the site is conditional on the number and quality of the profiles, because the value of a network increases according to the square law: double the connections and you quadruple the value;[26] 100% complete profiles encourage connections, and increase value.

How do they encourage users to spend time making their site more valuable?

They designed a profile completeness meter that looks both ways: backwards by telling you how much you've completed, and forwards by telling you what you need to complete to get to the next level. The feedback twangs our weakness for levels and challenges.

The proof? As soon as they pushed it live they saw users taking the time to fill out more of their profile.

Valuable feedback indeed.

15 Ask nothing – other than to go public

'Don't look at me in that tone of voice.'

Dorothy Parker, 1893–1967

In 1839 the Vienna General Hospital's two maternity clinics unwittingly set up an experiment that transformed medical practice forever. As was common at the time, maternity clinics offered free services to expectant mothers in return for allowing trainee midwives and doctors to practise procedures. In Vienna General the two clinics split the trainees by profession: midwives in one, doctors in the other.

For the following seven years the average infant mortality rate in the doctors' clinic was just under 10% compared to a mortality rate in the midwives' clinic of just over 2%.[1] This was common knowledge. Women would beg to get into the midwives' clinic – some so desperate they gave birth on the pavement outside rather than be admitted to the doctors' clinic. And, in the cruelest of ironies, even the pavement mortality rate was lower.

Ignaz Semmelweiss – a young trainee doctor – was determined to solve this problem.

The only difference he could find was the doctors' additional responsibilities in the morgue. They were regularly handling dead bodies as well as helping women give birth, often on the same shift. He put the high rate of infant mortality down to 'an der Hand klebende Cadavertheile' or hand-carried 'cadaverous particles'.[2] He proposed hand washing as a solution.

It worked.

It took years for his idea to be believed and widely implemented, but eventually he saw his discovery transform the survival-rate of children – and adults – all over the world. In honour of his achievement Austria issued a Semmelweiss postage stamp on the 100th anniversary of his death.

Over 160 years later you'd think we'd have this 'hand washing' thing down pat ('cadaverous particles' and all). Not so. In a study in UCLA Medical Center, hand washing hovered around the 50% mark.[3] They had been trying to increase the rate of hand washing for a while by using nurses to conduct audits on their peers. Apparently, there was '100% compliance' with washing, even though anecdotal evidence from patients – and staff who had been patients – claimed this was false.

To try and fix this, Rosenthal, Erbeznik, Padilla, Zaroda, Nguyen, and Rodriguez planned and documented a study of staff at the UCLA Medical Center using undergraduate students to carry out observations.[4]

Twenty of them simply observed and recorded the behaviour of practising medical staff, documenting up to 800 actions per month. One of the observations was hand washing. Everybody knew about the study, and knew their behaviour would be made public to clinicians, and departmental and hospital leadership.

Did this close the gap between reporting and reality?

Hand washing compliance – previously at 50% – rocketed to over 90%. Unlike in Semmelweiss's day, the trainee doctors became the solution, not the problem. As it turns out, we are pretty sensitive to our actions being observed.

The rather neutral statement from the study says that 'MAPS [Measure to Achieve Patient Safety] has been widely accepted by the clinical staff.'[5] Whether that means it is greeted with a grimace or a grin, there's little dispute that data collection drives at the heart of our fear of reputational damage.

Public behaviour is the forum in which social standards are set, and so behaviour that is invisible is necessarily removed from social consideration (favourable or not). In this case it was hand washing, but in a wider context resource-relieving behaviour – like sustainable energy supplies – is usually invisible to others. There is little need to ask anything, other than to instigate public consideration by, well, going public.

Public convenience

In a doctoral thesis by one of P. Wesley Schultz's students on cross-cultural comparisons of alcohol consumption, heavy drinkers in the USA, Germany, Mexico, and Japan were told how their boozing compared to their peers'. Above-average boozers said they would be influenced in different ways by this comparison: The Germans and Americans seemed proudly independent and said they would not be swayed; the Mexicans and Japanese typically value consensus and said they were happy to say they would be swayed. Despite what any said, or thought, all the above-average boozers reduced their drinking in line with average levels – they were all influenced by their peers.[6]

Anyone for a pint of social norms?

These four countries (USA, Germany, Mexico, Japan), and 138 more, are ranked in the Environmental Sustainability Index, which is the brainchild of Daniel C. Esty, a professor of Environmental Law from Yale, who was awarded by the American Bar Association in 2002 for the very same.

Publicly ranked across a spectrum of environmental concerns, such as air quality, biodiversity, and environmental governance, many countries respond competitively. Etsy says, 'there are competitive juices that flow. Nobody wants to be at the bottom of a ranking.'[7] And that ranking is based on rigorously tested data, and compares like-for-like measurements – Cameroon is not usefully compared with Canada, for instance.

Norway's Prime Minister responded to their second place (out of 142) by trying to find a fix instead of enjoying the ride: 'Rather than crowing about Norway's superb showing,' Etsy says, 'all he [the Prime Minister of Norway] wanted to talk about was what his country could do to overtake Finland and become number one.'[8]

And since the United Arab Emirates came last in 2002, they met with Esty and made a $5 million investment in the Abu Dhabi Global Initiative to improve environmental data collection. They've become converts to the empirical environmental measurement cause (or they just don't want to be last on the list). No one is changing the law, only making ranked performance public.

The Land of the Free, the Home of the Ranked

On 3 December 1984, Union Carbide was an international chemical manufacturing company largely unknown to the wider public. Nine months, later it had killed 2,500 people and injured over 200,000 more in India and the United States of America.

In two separate incidents, in their plants in Bhopal, India and Institute, West Virginia, highly toxic chemicals leaked into the air, causing confusion, damage, and death. They clearly showed how inadequate their emergency prevention measures were when both local authorities were confused about what was happening, what substance was involved, and how to protect citizens.

The 150 injuries in West Virginia was bad, but the 2,500 deaths in Bophal gave a forceful shove to the Comprehensive Environmental Response, Compensation, and Liability Act of 1980 (CERCLA) that was making baby-steps through the US Congress. It eventually ended up as the Emergency Planning and Community Right-to-Know Act of 1986 (EPCRA). Ronald Reagan signed it into US law with two aims: to encourage and support planning for chemical accidents; to give government and citizens local information about chemical hazards.

'This law seemed to be merely a bookkeeping measure',[9] say Thaler and Sunstein in the *Chicago Tribune*, but even so, the second part of the Act – 'the right-to-know' provision – was heavily opposed by industry and parts of the government. But it passed.

The EPCRA started out with a whimper, not a bang. And it remains rather obscure. But it has become one of the most successful pieces of environmental legislation in the USA in decades because of its 'right-to-know' provisions. They are described as 'among the most important weapons in efforts to combat pollution.',[10] and not (as you might assume) by environmentalists or a small group of activists, but by (the elder) Bush administration's Environmental Protection Agency administrator.

The first report revealed eye-opening data on the toxic releases and transfers into air, land, and water. The Pareto principle was broadly in evidence: of the 20,000 polluters, most were in a few States, from a few businesses, represented by a handful of chemicals. Terms like 'startling'[11] and 'staggering'[12] came out of government at the time, and the EPA said the pollution was 'far higher than we thought was going to occur.'[13]

The data is used by a wide variety of people: environmental organizations, government and legislative bodies, the press/media, and industry. *USA Today* used freshly released data in the late eighties for a special three-day series about toxic pollution to an audience of 2 million readers. This is now an annual press ritual. William K. Reilly (Administrator of the Environmental Protection Agency under President George H. W. Bush) says the data 'serves "as an eye opener to lots of CEOs" who find themselves embarrassed by the bad publicity created by the findings of the TRI reports'.[14]

There was no change in the law, only a change in the reporting of data that spurred large reductions in toxic releases at every level of the list. (Someone's always better than you, or worse, unless you're at the absolute top or bottom.) The 'go public' nature of this is like the hand-washing doctors scenario – but on steroids.

Rank outsiders

'Why are our competitors beating us in this category?', you will hear at some point in every boardroom. Except, these days, it's said more and more in reference to sustainability. Why?

Publicly listed businesses' performance is ruthlessly picked over, packaged, compared, and contrasted by the financial markets. So once one company 'falls for sustainability', as the *Harvard Business Review* describes it, 'it knocks the rest over too. And once the competitive green one-upsmanship [*sic*] gets going, it's hard to stop.'[15]

Wal-Mart, Marks & Spencer, and Best Buy all chase each other up and down their sustainable performance figures under the emotionless gaze of the investors because M&S 'tipped the first domino'. Wal-Mart are – like a lot of other retailers – peering their heads around the door marked 'suppliers' and asking (at the moment) rather nicely if they wouldn't mind awfully reducing their embedded carbon.[16] Their suppliers' carbon performance is playing havoc with their ranking, and – now this information is public – their market value too. UPS and FedEx are announcing tit-for-tat initiatives to become the most sustainable shipper. When FedEx introduced electric vehicles, UPS followed, but pointed out they'd been using them since the 1930s. The FedEx boss claims, 'UPS would not have set a reduction goal [of carbon dioxide] if we hadn't not it [*sic*] first'[17]

In Chapter 12, 'Ask with the right authority', I write up Ray Anderson's business, Interface, Inc., which is working to be carbon free. (And making great strides: they have cut total carbon dioxide emissions by over 60% and made 111 million square yards of climate-neutral carpet since 2003.) Gregory C. Unruh reports in the *Harvard Business Review* that: 'An executive from an Interface rival told me that their green product development efforts were spurred by senior executives who said, "We need a market response to Interface!"'[18]

There are many parts of a business that can tip the domino in favour of reducing resource-stress and resource-cost. Chris McKenna runs the fleet of delivery trucks for Poland Spring. After they'd been fitted with management software called the Driver Engine Usage Report to generate paperless logs for each truck and driver, he realized that he could also use this software to track engine idling time. He worked with the manufacturer to tap the data. Once they'd pulled it out, McKenna talked to all sixty-five drivers, ranked the results, and posted them in the break room.

'Driver behaviour started to change almost immediately . . . It's just human nature that no one wants to be at the bottom of the list',[19] McKenna says. But was their immediate change a significant change?

Between the start in 2007 and the latest released data from 2009, idling time has dropped by 70%.

'We didn't have to come up with elaborate rules',[20] says McKenna, to reduce 1,400 hours of idling. The driver ranking saved 77 tons of carbon dioxide per year, and reduced costs by $20,000 (2008 data). It's an impressive change. (Although it does also go to show just *how* much fuel a fleet uses if only part of the idling time equates to $20k of fuel.)

Indeed, McKenna achieved all this without creating an attitudinal change in his drivers: 'It's been a pretty awesome story . . . It's so simple. There are no other changes required than behavioural .'[21]

A similar outcome is documented in a paper called 'Changing organizational energy consumption behaviour through comparative feedback' by Siero, Bakker, Dekker, and Van Den Burg, in which they test public energy consumption data between two departments of a metallurgical firm.[22] In one department employees were asked to set energy conservation goals and received feedback on their efforts. The other department had the same, but with additional information about the performance of the other unit: they saved more energy. The authors say, 'A remarkable finding was that behavioural change took place with hardly any changes in attitudes or intentions.'[23]

I find it even more suprising that the comparative condition was saving energy, 'even half a year after the intervention'.[24]

––––––––––––––––––

Clearly, 'going public' changes behaviour by tapping into our deeply held sensitivity to being observed as well as our desire to avoid losing, but more broadly it describes what's 'normal' and tells each participant where they sit on that scale. These norms drive our behaviour in ways few of us would like to admit – especially the boozers who insisted they're influenced little by others' boozing habits – but they are an important part of our make-up, and shouldn't be seen as weakness, or fault. In fact, they pretty much kept us alive for thousands of years: It was dangerous being an outsider because that affected your chance of survival (in a bad way). And while that life is long gone, and we are safer than we've ever been (in the developed countries, at least), still no one wants to be the odd-ball.

Especially in public.

A clean win

In December 1997 the Los Angeles County government required restaurants to display publicly their hygiene inspection grade cards. They were the same ones they'd received for years from the Department of Health Services (DHS).

Public display was the only change.

Ginger Zhe Jin and Phillip Leslie, of the Universities of Maryland and Stanford respectively, studied the effects of this increased information in the area codes affected.[25] They gathered real-world data on hospital admissions and business turnover alongside the hygiene rating.

The results were positive, and pervasive.

They found A-grade ratings increased from nearly 60% to over 80% – probably because the financial penalties and gains were becoming obvious to the restauranteurs: C-graded restaurants lost custom, but those moving from a B-grade to an A-grade saw revenue up by 5% on average.

But that wasn't all. The health of customers increased too: 'The finding that grade cards reduce illnesses is fairly striking.'[26] Especially when you consider hospitalizations decreased by up to 20%.

Going public, going well.

16 Ask for it back

'Possession is nine points of the law.'

Unattributed, fifteenth century

If I ask you to give me something you own, in order to fulfil my request you'll have to give it up. You might do so, or you might not. It depends on how much you value 'it' (including not at all), and how much compensation you need to secure a suitable (perfect or imperfect) substitute. It seems I'm stating the obvious. And I would forgive you for admonishing me for the very same, but all's not well in the 'possession' camp; it's complicated.

We have a gap.

A gap that says we value losses higher than equivalent gains. A gap that says we want more to give 'it' up than we are willing to pay to acquire 'it'. A gap that says 'asking for something back' appears to strengthen the owner's grip. A gap that says the pain of giving back is greater than the pleasure of getting.

A gap called the 'Endowment effect'.

It says we place a higher value on owned items over un-owned items. This suggests the effect can only be evoked using items *already* owned: this is true. But 'items already owned' is a larger pool than commercial products. We 'own' laws, customs, and services – and even 'defaults'. They, too, are ours. And we feel the pang of loss if they're taken from us.

To paraphrase the ad man David Ogilvy, defaults are not a standing army, but a marching parade.[1] Through the years, different parts of society become relevant to us – different defaults are presented, adopted, and accepted. We own a lot more 'stuff' than we acknowledge. And we soon notice if it's taken away.

Ned Welch, writing in the *McKinsey Quarterly*, shows us just how subtle ownership can be. He describes an Italian telecoms company who offered 100 free calls to cellphone customers who phoned to quit the service. It wasn't very successful.

So they switched the presentation, but not the content, of their offer to: 'We have already credited your account with 100 calls – how could you use those?'[2] This was much more successful because, he says, 'Many customers did not want to give up free talk time they felt they already owned.'[3] The telecoms company put customers in a position where they would have to give back calls in order to quit; and who wants to do that?

'Asking for something back' evokes ownership. Ownership is the main condition of the Endowment effect. And the Endowment effect says we don't want to give it up. And around we go.

Hold the line please caller. Your call is important to us.
We will be with you shortly . . .

Natural response

In Chapter 6, 'Ask – but have a default option', I talk about Daniel Pichert and Konstantinos Katsikopoulos from the Max Planck Institute's investigation into our response to default electricity supplies. As part of their suite of experiments they also looked into the effects of endowment in real-world situations. It is all too easy to construct experiments where choice is made 'clean' without any incumbents: life isn't like that. For instance, when we move house we often pick up whatever utilities are already there. This is a form of endowment. To test its strength, Pichert and Katsikopoulos looked at how willing people would be to give up different types of electricity supply.[4]

What happens when you ask for it back?

A group of participants in their twenties were given a short description of the different types of electricity generation and how they worked in practice. This preceded questions about their willingness to switch supplies, and how much they would pay, or have to be compensated by, in order to do so. (Those that refused to switch for ideological reasons were removed from the study.) Those that were prepared to consider switching were asked to 'try different numbers' in their heads before committing to an answer.

The first group was given a grey electricity supply. They were told a 'grey' supply – commonly called conventional electricity – is generated by the burning of fossil fuels (like coal) and atomic power.

This group was asked to imagine they lived in a city supplied with conventional grey electricity, and told they were free to switch to a green supply if they wished, but switching meant a higher monthly bill. If they wanted to switch they were asked the maximum additional amount they would be willing to pay each month. This gives a good indication of our willingness to pay for a change to an existing condition (which of course can be zero).

In decision-making research, the 'willingness to pay' condition is contrasted with the 'willingness to accept' condition – and this is how the second group was tested.

The second group was asked to imagine they lived in a city supplied with green electricity, and told they were free to switch to a grey supply if they wished, and switching meant a lower monthly bill. If they wanted to switch they were asked how much cheaper it would need to be for them to consider.

This gives a good indication of our willingness to accept a change to an existing condition.

The results were asymmetric: While the grey-supply group were willing to pay an average of nearly €7 extra per month for a green supply, the green-supply group demanded nearly €13 to give it up.

In a rational world the two outcomes should be similar – or even the same. But it seems 'asking for it back' shows us the premium we place on ownership, even when it's a donated ownership. In this instance our behaviour is not characterized by limp acceptance, but rather by a desire to protect what we have. As Pichert and Katsikopoulos say, 'once a green [supply] . . . is established, people are either reluctant to move away from this reference point or they demand a relatively large sum to do so'.[5]

Endowment seems to affect greatly our reactions to environmental risks and losses, particularly with choices that have irreversible outcomes. Boyce, Brown, McClelland, Peterson, and Schulze tested this using a small Norfolk Island pine tree as their bait: asking volunteers to submit bids to either purchase a pine tree (which they could use as a house plant) or sell a pine tree they were given (back to the study team). The wrinkle being, all pine trees not purchased by the volunteers (in the willingness to purchase condition) or all pine trees not kept (in the willingness to accept condition) would be – as they say in the study paper – 'killed by the experimenter'.[6]

The kernel of this exchange is the death of trees that were either the property of the experimenter or the property of the volunteer. Yours or mine?

If the tree was the experimenters' the average purchase price to avoid the 'kill' was nearly $8. If the tree was the volunteers' the average price to sell for the kill was over $18. The volunteers wanted over twice as much to compensate for killing 'their' tree.

Boyce *et al.* feel they captured a sense of moral responsibility inherent in the killing of a pine tree – a proxy for environmental damage or species eradication. More fundamentally, the framing of ownership defined the property-rights allocation, which acted as a catalyst for moral responsibility. So whoever had the responsibility was the author of a 'needless' death.

Have someone own it, and then ask for it back.

Cass Sunstein, a Harvard law professor, discusses environmental ownership in terms of a legal bequest, rather than a physical object, in the form of air quality surrounding a railroad.[7]

It is correct to say that no legal system can function without clearly stating the rights of those it affects. For instance, those in democracies are endowed with the presumption of innocence. There are many others. Some are local and comparatively trivial – you can park here between 8 a.m. and 6 p.m. at weekends – but the effect of the initial allocation of rights is incredibly significant, irrespective of the significance or triviality of their outcome.

Take Sunstein's example of a railroad and its permission to emit air pollution. Should the right to pollute go to the railroad? Or should the right to clean air go to the track-side residents? Ronald Coase's theorem – the

Coase theorem – was developed as a response to problems with the law of tort (the disputes between individuals rather than between individuals and society). It states the initial allocation of rights casts no shadow on the final agreement between those two parties. In the railroad example, for instance, it makes no difference if the railroad's allowed to pollute, or if the residents are allowed clean air – whatever compensation or exchanges that can take place between those parties will, and the allocation of the compensation will be subsequently efficient.[8]

But the endowment effect says not.[9] Irrespective of where the rights are allocated, both parties value them asymmetrically, and immediately. Sunstein explains: 'People to whom the entitlement has been initially allocated will value it most . . . because of the initial allocation. For example, a grant of the initial entitlement to breathers will probably make them value clean air more than they otherwise would.'[10]

In opposition to the Coase theorem, allocation is important.

But here's the rub: in a situation where you don't know what society's preference is, and knowing that endowment confers an asymmetric valuation, how do you correctly allocate environmental rights? Evidently, it's easy with a neutral start-point, but we are not afforded that privilege. Here's the double rub: if there are rights to confer, and you know they will skew valuation, on which side do you fall? What are the checks and balances? *Quis custodiet ipsos custodes*: who guards the guards?

But then, maybe climate challenges and the alleviation of stress on resources like water and ground quality are not comprised of such dark and stark decisions.

Less than a decade ago a Yale conference called 'Americans and Climate Change: Closing the Gap between Science and Action' wondered – amongst other things – what form communications should take to get a better response to climate change. Frankly, they drew a blank. That may be a little uncharitable, but their smörgåsbord of approaches – including practical solutions – implied a lack of consensus. There was one nugget, however: the proclamation that future communications approaches should be centred around the decision *either* to spend money now to mitigate future effects of climate change *or* to spend money later adapting to unchecked climate change – rather than the current situation which presents *either* a 'do nothing' status quo *or* spend money later adapting to unchecked climate change.[11]

The 'do nothing status quo *or* spend money' pairing is the foundation of discussions about whether climate change is happening or not: more common in pubs and bars than it is amongst scientists, government, and business. The 'cost now *or* cost later' scenario is more representative of current scientific debate, and business-to-business discussions, in that it says we are already endowed with climate change. The Yale conference had understood that the presentation of the debate defines the endowed position, and the value therein.

A fact to which the allocation of rights, pine trees, electricity supplies, and free cellphone talk minutes can attest.

We are experiencing unexpected call volume.
Please hold the line . . .

Mug's game

One of the go-to experiments for behavioural economists in demonstration of the endowment effect is Daniel Kahneman, Jack Knetsch, and Richard Thaler's 'mugs' test from a series of mugs, pens, and tokens experiments.[12]

They randomly assign mugs to one third of the participants. Those with a mug are cast as *sellers* and those without are split evenly and cast as either *buyers* or *choosers*. When they are asked to price the mugs from a menu ranging from below the shop price ($0.25) to way above ($9.25), the *choosers* and *buyers* assign similar cash values, but the *sellers* assign much higher values. It is evident that the *sellers'* reluctance to sell is not a condition of the *buyers'* unwillingness to part with a fair amount of money – something we conclude from the *choosers'* similar valuation as 'independent adjudicators' – but an unwillingness on the part of the seller to reach a similar valuation because of their original endowment. Kahneman, Knetsch, and Thaler propose: 'the low volume of trade is produced mainly by owners' reluctance to part with their endowment, rather than by buyers' unwillingness to part with their cash.'[13] Their view of the mugs' value is inflated by being viewed through the prism of the endowment effect.

I introduce this experiment not to tread a worn path but to extend it into Brosnan, Jones, Lambeth, Mareno, Richardson, and Schapiro's similar endowment experiment with chimpanzees, peanut butter, and frozen fruit juice.[14] (I wouldn't want to be there.)

The chimps were fed and watered, and free-tested for their preference towards peanut butter and frozen juice. About 60% preferred the peanut butter leaving just over 40% preferring the juice. They ran this test three more times and preferences were within a couple of percentage points each time: the chimps had spoken.

Then all were given peanut butter and encouraged to swap it for juice with one of the human testers. They tried the opposite too (all given juice and encouraged to swap for peanut butter). The chimps' preferences shouldn't change from their previous 'free' selection. But, no dice. Or not much dice anyhow: the peanut butter preference rose from nearly 60% to nearly 80%, and the juice preference rose from nearly 40% to nearly 60%. They were swapping less frequently because they 'owned' their treat – even though they had no role in choosing it.[15] This near 20% increase due to endowment compares with an over 30% 'stick-not-twist' endowment behaviour for us humans in 'mug' tests.[16]

Chimps were tested with additional items like bone and rope. They swap-tested all four of the items with an identical object. None swapped peanut butter for the same; few did so with juice. But they all swapped the bone and rope for the same – the interaction with the experimenter seemed to be the reward rather than the object itself. This suggests, 'the effect is far stronger for food than for less evolutionarily salient objects, perhaps due to historically greater risks associated with keeping a valuable item versus attempting to exchange it for another'.[17]

But then endowment effect reared its head again in intra-food swaps: a tester's large frozen fruit stick was not always swapped for an endowed bite-sized piece, and endowed peanut butter was not always swapped for a much more preferable tester's banana. This 'frequent failure to exchange a less-favoured food for a more-preferred food was an active choice to maintain possession of the food item. This is consistent with human behaviour that has been interpreted as an endowment effect.'[18]

Unsurprisingly, food-based monkey-business is not exclusive to the laboratory. Surprisingly, it isn't exclusive to monkeys: Frank Bruni saw it in the wild when he was the *New York Times*' food critic.

Frank would typically take three friends to New York restaurants in order to sample large numbers of dishes without raising suspicion. His rules for his undercover guests were simple: they ordered what they're told, and then everyone gets to taste an equal portion. Who *actually* ordered what was irrelevant. Indeed, Frank would say: 'Remember, you're all just temporary custodians of the dish you're asking for.'[19] But even so, the 'temporary custodianship' instruction soon mutated into a partiality towards their original order, even though they had no role in choosing it.

'Each guest seemed to think that what he or she wound up ordering was a matter of identity, a reflection of self. And more often than not . . . would go on to describe and defend that dish as the very best',[20] says Frank.

His experience is that ownership is evoked even when the 'ownership' is decided randomly. This is exactly what Johnson, Häubl, and Keinan found when they were investigating Query Theory: 'the value of an object depends on ownership, even when that ownership is assigned randomly'.[21]

Your call is important to us.
We will be with you shortly . . .

At the owner's expense

Along with the allocation of rights, pine trees, electricity supplies, cellphones, chimpanzees' tea parties, and New York meals, endowment can cost decision-makers a lot of money – be they individuals or entire countries.

In 1985, Hersh Shefrin and Mere Statman looked into why traders and businesses tend to sell winning stocks too early and hold losers too long, even though all the market signals were 'asking for it back'.[22] This was true for businesses that bought smaller companies that turned out to be poor investments, for product development choices that went sour (Lockheed's folly with a new plane had the market screaming so loudly for the loss to be realized the stock rose by 18% the day they finally killed the project), and for individuals managing private retirement funds (more common in the USA). The regret of realizing a loss is greater than the pride of realizing a gain.

I think, in hindsight, the ex-Prime Minister of Great Britain, Tony Blair would recognize that condition in relation to his handling of a large government-funded project already underway when he took office to build an entertainment and celebration space in London for the millennium celebrations, called the Millennium Dome. He says, 'by the time we took office around £100 million had been committed, so cancellation costs would have been significant'.[23] This is true, but the final bill came in at nearly 1 billion pounds, and the structure was sold at a loss to a commercial company. If he was trying to save money by continuing with the project, he didn't. The country would've realized a smaller loss had he pulled the plug when he had the chance. This is not to say that he should have pulled the project, rather that the fear of loss is not sufficient *logical* ammunition to continue spending.

Realizing a loss under public scrutiny is even harder than a private one, perhaps. An important part of endowment is the crystallization of losses – it's almost impossible to make them real, if you haven't made peace with them. Cass Sunstein encapsulates the thought succinctly: 'An especially influential approach to the endowment effect stresses "loss aversion," which refers to the fact that a negative change from the status quo is usually seen as more harmful than a positive change is seen as beneficial.'[24]

You can mitigate these effects by creating time and distance between the object and the decision maker, but this isn't always practical.

Endowment effects on long-held or high-value intellectual and physical property make sense. But baffling to all are the effects produced by the duration-of-exposure and length-of-ownership effects when they are reduced to astonishingly small durations.

We can evoke endowment when we 'ask for it back' even after an object is touched for a few seconds. In an adaptation of the mug experiment, participants were given $10 and told they would soon see a brand new mug to examine with a price tag of $4.99.[25] They were sorted into bidding pairs. Half of the pairs were given the mug to examine for 10 seconds each, and then began to bid against each other for the mug. It was the same for the other half of the pairs, except they examined the mug for 30 seconds. It was an English bid (highest price wins) lasting 15 minutes with a soft ending (a bid in the last 15 seconds extends the auction by 15 additional seconds, and 15 bid-free seconds must pass before the auction can close).

The average winning bid for the 10-second group was $3.70, versus $5.80 for the 30-second group. (Not forgetting the seen price tag of $4.99.)

James Wolf, Hal Arkes, and Waleed Muhanna – the authors of the experiment – very clearly tell us (correctly) that 'caution should be exercised before generalizing these results to longer durations of exposure',[26] but they are (correctly) comfortable citing examples from big retail: 'It is partially for this reason [exposure] that GM and other automobile companies offer 24-hour test drives to their customers.'[27] And they remind us that pet shops often have play areas for puppies, and bookshops have seating and coffee areas to 'read before you buy'. Which I'd postulate is more correctly described as 'feel a sense of ownership before you buy'.

Almost all of the major motor manufacturers are making variations of fossil-fuel-minimized or -free cars, and it's the dealers that are traditionally the interface between your cash and their cars. However, it looks like someone from the PR side at Nissan has a grasp on the endowment effect and has employed it on the UK demonstration tour of the Nissan LEAF. In the promotional material they say: 'Be in with a chance to win our prize draw of a Nissan LEAF for one month when you book a driving experience on the tour.'[28] That will evoke the endowment effect, for sure, but it's a shame it's worked so only one person can try a donor vehicle.

You are second in line.
A representative will be with you shortly . . .

We started out with a great example of environmental psychology at work where Pichert and Katsikopoulos found that 'participants were willing to pay a small premium for green electricity but demanded considerably more in compensation for giving up the green electricity supply'.[29] Endowment in this instance, and the others discussed, seems to be consistently exhibited by those in the ownership condition, whether that ownership is long- or short-term, real or imagined. (What's the difference anyway?) But stability of endowment can be affected.

It is possible that output interference – which inhibits memory retrieval – and retrieval-induced forgetting (A relates to C more easily than A relates to B, so focus on A recollects C)[30] can affect the strength of the endowment effect because, as Johnson, Häubl, and Keinan suggest, we consider the advantage of the current state – ownership – before considering the disadvantages of the new state – loss.[31] This order in which we query a question that 'asks for it back' can account for endowment, and if it is constructed by query order, it can be manipulated and in some cases neutralized.[32]

They discovered this with a mugs-redux experiment in which respondents inspected a mug, gave it back, and then gave it a price after listing either value-increasing or value-decreasing aspects of the mug.[33] The expectation was that the price would fall or rise in line with the value aspects respondents were asked to list. It did. The difference was about 40% higher for the value-increasing listees.

Reordering question-sequences at first seems to undermine the endowment effect, but it only goes to show its psychological basis, and its effect on our decision-making. But, manipulable or not, Kahneman, Knetsch, and Thaler summarize it thus: 'the main effect of endowment is not to enhance the appeal of the good one owns, only the pain of giving it up'.[34]

So once you've identified an action that relieves resource-stress and 'asked for it back', the pain of having to give it up will highlight its endowed value. And if it isn't already owned, you can endow it by considering its presentation.

Welcome.
Please select the phone tariff you'd like to use
with your free 100 calls per month . . .

Part V

The swerves

All the wrong questions, all the right answers

Albert Einstein is the author of some extraordinary thinking: he has transformed the way we think about the universe and our place in it. But I think one of his most insightful ideas relates to his approach to problems: 'We cannot solve our problems with the same thinking we used when we created them.'

And this is where we meet 'The swerves'.

Swerves that tell us that in China's 'Warring States' period, Pang Cong understood enough about swerves to tell his ruling monarch that 'three men make a tiger' rather than begging for a remembered legacy. And the swerves tell us the importance of 'don't leave the campfire' versus 'stay with the campfire'. (The tigers didn't start it.) They also give us the 'Lisbon stairs', the grey area between having and not having, and the prevention of habits with the behavioural lock-in.

The swerves tell us how on Sunday, 30 April 1916, Kaiser Wilhelm II stood on the (metaphorical) shoulders of Benjamin Franklin to make incredible efficiency savings in every German home and business at the stroke of a pen – and how that simultaneously created the reason we all risk being late, or early, for appointments on the same two days every year.

You'll like the swerves – no question.

17 Ask a different question

'A sudden bold and unexpected question doth many times surprise a man and lay him open.'

Sir Francis Bacon, 1561–1626

In the heart of the Portuguese capital city Lisbon, on Rua dos Correeiros – a pedestrian street not far from the train station and the coast – is a small, friendly, second-floor backpackers' rest-stop called the Goodnight Hostel. It's a bustling place jammed into a classic southern European city townhouse – it has a flat stone front, large windows, and small wrought iron balconies.

As is customary in hotels and hostels spread over a number of floors, they have an elevator and stairs. The stairs are different from most. On the vertical face of each step there is a calorific value inscribed. The Goodnight Hostel calculates climbing each step equates to 0.004 calories of effort, and presents it as a cumulative total in ascending order up the staircase.[1]

It is a novel way of asking patrons for consideration with energy use: instead of baldly asking 'Will you take the stairs to reduce our electricity use?', they imply instead a question that entices the calorie conscious and fitness aware to use the stairs.

Both approaches drive to the same outcome – lower electricity use – but they come at it from different angles. This is the genesis of 'asking a different question'.

Are there any other 'Lisbon stairs' questions out there?

Driving choice

Do you need a car?

Most people's answer to the question 'do you need a car?' is 'yes'. Dig further and you find out most people need their car at least some of the time for journeys that are difficult to replace with another form of transport. The number of times unsubstitutable private transport is needed generally increases the further you travel from cities. But the 'do you need a car?'

question only allows an answer of 'yes' or 'no'. It's a pretty stark choice, and doesn't account for the fact that for some journeys there are alternatives – a walk to the newsagents, and a sleeper-train to another city – and for others there are few – a supermarket trip, a late-night dash to the chemist. As David Uzzell, Professor of Environmental Psychology at the University of Surrey, UK, says in conversation with Leo Hickman of the *Guardian* newspaper in reference to juggling the demands of life in the face of government edicts to drive on fewer short trips: 'We need to change the conditions rather than attack individual behaviours.' [2]

Change which conditions?

Do you need all of a car?

A hire car. That's the solution to this question. Done. Although there is a modification to the hire car model that makes it feel more like you're sharing a car and less like you're hiring someone else's: car clubs

Zipcar is the world's largest pay-as-you-go car club. It's a simple membership scheme where cars are available to hire for as little as thirty minutes to as long as six months, although most people use them for the shorter end of the scale. For a short-hire to work it needs to be conveniently located, so Zipcar leaves its cars in specified parking spaces around cities. The original tag-line echoes this: 'Wheels when you want them'. An upside for the business is the removal of costly car-hire shops.

Two friends who strongly believed in car-sharing as a way to help protect the environment founded Zipcar in 1999. One of the original partners, Danielson, was a carbon-emissions researcher and viewed car-sharing as a way to reduce carbon emissions. She and the other founder, Chase, are no longer with the company since Griffith came in and grew it from a principled start-up to the business behemoth it is today.

Interestingly, Griffith said in an interview with *Inc.* magazine, 'I don't think people are going to use Zipcar because it's green',[3] which goes back to the heart of asking the right question of your audience – i.e. 'Do you want a bit of a car? (And a bit of the cost?)', instead of 'Do you want to do your bit for the environment?' Nonetheless, the marquee environmental stats for Zipcar (via the UK-based 'Streetcar', which they now own) state that every car they add takes fifteen individually owned cars off the road.[4] A quick-and-dirty bit of maths gives us a usage figure of about 6.7% of a car.

Do you need a car all of the time?

Technically, no. Whipcar realized this could be a business, so set-up the world's first 'neighbour-to-neighbour' car rental service. Yep – you can hire your car out to your neighbour. (Or anyone, in fact.) Their service provides an insurance policy that supersedes the owner's, and other stuff that makes it work – but the point is they ask a variation on the 'Zipcar' question: 'Now you've got a car, and you realize it sits around a lot, d'you wanna make a few quid out of it?'

Necessarily this rules out groups where car ownership is low (due to income, age, etc.), and groups where wealth is high (the costs of motoring are much less of a burden), but there is a substantial middle ground according to the *Sunday Times* newspaper in the UK: 'Nearly half (46%) of households drive less than 5,000 miles a year, and with 29m registered car owners in the UK there is clearly a great deal of spare capacity available.'[5]

If proof were needed that this is a mainstream idea rather than a well-meaning backwater, Mike Senackerib from Hertz in the US says: 'There's a market for car-sharing and it's larger than has been developed to date.'[6] And it's not only US- and UK-centric – Susan Shaheen and Elliot Martin of Berkeley, California have researched Chinese attitudes towards car-sharing, finding it has positive 'appeal across the socio-demographic groups'.[7] There are some challenges: appeal is skewed towards a younger demographic; 40% of the respondents weren't aware of the concept.

I present this as an example of how far you can go simply by asking a different question, rather than proposing car-sharing per se (remembering I'm writing about choice architecture rather than the choices themselves). However, it seems the car-sharing example I've used is not just 'stuff' happening at the edges.

The major motor manufacturers are getting in on the act.

Volkswagen have launched a car-sharing service in the German city of Hanover, BMW have a tie-up in Munich, and Daimler have a presence in Ulm and Hamburg in Germany, and in Austin, Texas in the USA. Peugeot also have car-sharing services in British, French, and German cities.[8]

One of the unintended consequences of car-sharing is increasing fossil-fuel car use by introducing the non-car-owning population. But this needn't be a problem – Parisians have an electric car rental service similar to the Zipcar model with ultra short-term rental periods (they seem to be continuing a tradition that dates back to 1940s Europe) and Daimler have an EV-sharing programme in Amsterdam.

As the *Independent* newspaper in the UK, says: 'Last year, business analyst Frost & Sullivan predicted that 5.5 million Europeans will be part of a car sharing scheme in 2016, with every third vehicle added to the schemes from next year likely to be electric.'[9]

Hot in here

Household temperature. It's one of the simplest and commonest interfaces we have with energy consumption, and yet it's wrapped in one of the most complex examples of behavioural influence. Construal Level Theory's four dimensions of influence describe consequences that are either: 'here' or some degree of 'not here'; 'now' or some degree of 'not now'; 'acting on me' or some degree of 'acting on someone else'; 'clear in outcome' or some degree of 'unclear in outcome'.[10]

We make decisions about room temperature on the clear and personal end of the scale in all four dimensions: how warm is it here, right now, according to me, based on the temperature I feel? Those decisions about room temperature have consequences that are opposite in every one of the four dimensions: the effects of increased energy consumption are felt elsewhere, not now, by someone else, in a way that is ill defined (climate change, oil spills, cost of transport, etc.).

This 'perfect storm' leaves us all peering through a glass, darkly. Can we make it clearer?

What temperature do you want?

'What temperature do you want?' is the question asked by almost every thermostat control dial on every home in the western world. It's a fair question, because it refers to what it does – change the temperature. But that's not necessarily the best way for us to engage. Indeed, of all the ways in which we engage with modern technology, this is right up there as one of the most confusing because it's couched in a spaghetti-mess of behavioural reinforcements acting to the detriment of the environment.

'What temperature are the Jones's?'

Group-level feedback similar to the Ambient Orb electricity meter can tell the user what temperature is common in their neighbourhood, or office. This is similar to Opower's electricity billing service which shows users how much they are consuming compared to their neighbours. This use of social norms can be powerful. Norms do fluctuate, but usually over generations: in Georgian times having a warm house meant you were a generous person – the profligacy was evidence you had more than enough resources not to worry about a little waste. In medieval times profligacy was a sign of madness because heat and light were prohibitively expensive – a popular saying of the time was 'Is the game worth the candle?'[11]

'What price do you want to pay?'

One could ask 'what price do you want to pay?', and have the thermostat bid for electricity under the price specified. That idea might leave you a bit cold, but the price needn't be financial; it could be environmental, and it could be measured in a way specified by the user. You could even wrap the financial and environmental together, which is what the Carbon Reduction Commitment does (by measuring a business's carbon output, allocating shares, and allowing trading on the open market with other businesses in the scheme).

For some, the price they want to pay is zero. A survey by the *Air-Conditioning, Heating & Refrigeration News* discovered fifty-one out of seventy respondents had installed a dummy thermostat on an air-conditioning unit in an office at the request of the landlord or the businesses.[12] (I had no idea placebo was so widespread.)

A lot of these examples are a combination of technological and infrastructural solutions, which is about as far as I want to go in service of highlighting the premise that asking different questions has value – a value that is measured by its ability to 'unpack' our heuristics.

But why do they need unpacking?

Habitual questioning

Schäfer and Bamberg tell us that that consumption patterns of food and mobility are often born of habit,[13] and habitual behaviour can be 'considered as a form of behavioural lock-in,' says Kevin Maréchal in his paper 'An Evolutionary Perspective on the Economics of Energy Consumption: The Crucial Role of Habits'.[14] This behavioural 'lock-in' affects the performance of incentives, which I'm sure will prick the ears of marketers and governments. Maréchal continues: 'The existence of habits in domestic energy consumption will most likely limit the effectiveness of incentives'[15] and Martiskaïnen adds colour by saying habits make an actor 'act opposite to his or her intentions without even realising it'.[16] This can be considered as a consequence of the 'Four horsemen of Automaticity', as John Bargh usefully describes it.[17] The constituents are: lack of control; lack of awareness; efficiency (rules of thumb); lack of intention.

Ascribing the simplest and most repetitive tasks to habit relieves us from the burden of making every decision from scratch. Once liberated, the best of our attention can be focused on urgent and important matters like avoiding being eaten by a lion or ambushed by an enemy (even though these 'urgent and important matters' are out-dated). This was discussed as far back as 1890 in William James's *The Principles of Psychology*.[18] Today, keeping our cognitive load light via the use of habits is just as beneficial (if not life-or-death) because, as Maréchal says, 'the constraints of today's society (i.e., the feeling of time pressure as well as the information overload) tend to favour the use of habits'.[19]

Disrupting habitual behaviour is the key to allowing us to make cognitive decisions, rather than instinctive decisions. It makes sense – who wouldn't want to be making a rational, considered opinion? (As much as one can in this mind-bending contextual-spaghetti of a world of ours.)

Disruption doesn't have to be in the form of a macro lever-and-pulley tech-frastructure or govern-tax. For one, it happens naturally to household consumption decisions and travel planning when people move house (more of a timing issue than a general fix, see Chapter 4, 'Ask at the right time'). As Tim Cotter says in conversation with Greg Foyster, 'Fixed conditions hold habits in place, so if you change those conditions, you can help change the habit.'[20]

Whilst changing the physical context is rarely tractable, the mental context can be changed by coming at the problem from a different angle – by asking a different question – and in doing so can arrest automaticity by requiring us to engage greater cognitive resources. These 'greater resources' once focused on the task at hand can afford us the opportunity to be aware of alternatives. Says Maréchal, 'breaking existing habits will require change in environmental cues and/or induced deliberation while time and repetition will be needed to promote alternative habitual behaviour'.[21]

Habit forming is commonly cited as needing approximately twenty-one days to bed-in, but this is a myth,[22] possibly the child of a study that reported a twenty-one day healing rate for broken bones that found its way to the self-help community via Chinese Whispers ('Send me three and four'pence I'm going to a dance/Send me reinforcements I'm going to advance'). Phillippa Lally's study into habit forming at University College London showed test subjects needed somewhere between almost twenty and over 250 days to form a habit that could be repeated every day. The average was about seventy days.[23]

Disruptive messaging lay at the heart of marketing as we know it, and it's something the industry's very good at – certainly better than the rather clumsy and often dictatorial disruptive messaging common to government. But it is only by having our habits disrupted that we get a chance to make informed decisions about them, rather than relying on our folded-packed-and-sealed habits of which the origins are long forgotten (this makes no provision for cognitive decisions to be in favour of one thing or another, simply that they're considered).

There are few simpler, persistent, and costless ways to disrupt and ask for consideration of a habit than to ask a different question.

(There's no question about that.)

18 Don't ask (tell)

'To do exactly as your neighbors do is the only sensible rule.'

Emily Post

Qin Shihuangdi first ruled China in 221 BC. He was the first Emperor, and laid the foundations for the world's oldest continuous political entity. However, the preceding two hundred years could not have been more different. Named the 'Warring States Period', it was characterized by a disunited collection of fractious power-bases, border raids, mass wars, and political turmoil. From this period we get the apocryphal story of 'sān rén chéng hǔx', or 'three men make a tiger'.

Pang Cong was an official of the central state of Wei and was, along with the king of Wei's son, part of a hostage swap-deal with the newly befriended neighbouring state of Zhao. Pang Cong – a talented minister – was worried about a whispering campaign against him while he was away.

He illustrated the problem to his king with a hypothetical situation: If one person says a tiger is roaming the streets of the capital, would the king believe him? No, says the king. Pang asks him, if he hears the same from two people, would he believe them? Again, no, says the king. Pang asks him, if three people say there is a tiger roaming the streets of the capital, would he believe them? The king says yes, with three people saying the same thing he would believe it. And with that, Pang reminded him that a tiger roaming the streets of the capital is absurd, but if enough people say so, it becomes true even without any evidence.

The voice of a 'gang' is strong: Pang knew this.

He told the king that although he was a talented and faithful minister, he had more than three enemies in court and, if 'three men make a tiger', could three men make him a bad minister? The king of Wei understood what Pang Cong meant, and sent him off on the hostage swap-deal, promising to remember his abilities whatever he heard about him in the royal court.

I think we can say that Pang Cong was a clever minister, if only because he understood and illustrated the power of social norms – the 'gang' – to his king more than 2,000 years ago.

This type of 'normative' behaviour states that we adjust our actions and opinions according to others'. There's nothing wrong with that. In fact, it's a pretty good strategy for staying alive: if 'they're' not eating it, I won't eat it; If 'they're' not going there, I won't go there; etc. It allows us to navigate the world efficiently by removing the need to employ costly cognitive load to work out what to do every time we're presented with a new choice.

In essence, we 'borrow' conclusions already established by others.

Because of this, if a 'norm' is a desirable behaviour, it is often much more powerful to tell people how many other people conform, rather than to ask for change. You really do very little work other than shine a light on an existing practice.

Norms are as pervasive and widespread today as they were in China over 2,000 years ago.

When in Rome

When in Rome, do as the Romans do, they say. Good advice. Better would be to do as they do in Phoenix, Arizona. Or more specifically, it would be better to do as they do in one particular upscale hotel in Phoenix, Arizona. (As a proverb, it won't catch on – it scans terribly for a start.)

Noah Goldstein, Robert Cialdini, and Vladas Griskevicius noticed an increasing number of hotels asking guest to consider reusing bath towels. It has obvious benefits for a hotel's bottom line: reducing laundry saves on labour costs, water, energy, and detergent. And it has an obvious benefit for the environment: resources – like water – are less stressed, and detergent pollution is reduced.[1]

However, despite the obvious benefits, and the 'nearly limitless array of angles to play and motivational strings to pull'[2] available to the marketing community, towel reuse messages all ploughed the same (unproductive) furrow: they were variations on the passive-aggressive 'crying dolphins'/'murderer!' type messages. Goldstein, Cialdini, and Griskevicius were sure there were more potent ways of eliciting a response. Existing industry data (in the USA) showed that the majority of guests already reused their towels at least once,[3] so maybe they could test messages that built on this 'norm'?

With the collaboration of a well-known US hotel chain, they put together a couple of experiments that involved hanging towel reuse cards on towel-rails (similar in size and shape as 'Do not disturb' door-knob hangers). Hotel staff were engaged in collecting towels, and those unclear about what constituted a reuse indication (on the floor, on a door handle, on a door hanger, etc.) were not part of the experiment. If anything, the results err on the side of caution.

The first experiment pitted the industry standard message against a 'normative' message. The industry standard towel-rail card was titled with 'Help Save the Environment' and continued with information stressing 'respect for nature' in some way. The normative message followed a descriptive pattern, 'Join Your Fellow Citizens in Helping to Save the Environment' and then gave information that 'the majority of hotel guests do reuse their towels more than once'.

The descriptive message returned nearly 45% reuse compared to the 35% of the standard version. A clear win for the 'descriptive norm' – messages that describe what everyone else is doing. A version of 'three men make a lion' (except not hypothetical).

The second experiment again pitted the standard message ('Help Save the Environment') against variations on the descriptive norm ('Join Your Fellow Citizens . . .'), using a variety of sub-descriptions from gender specific, to citizen specific, and 'other guest' related. But the most effective was the room-specific sub-description 'the guests who stayed in this room No. 304 participated in' – where 'No. 304' was their *actual* room number. This created a nearly 50% towel reuse rate. Clearly the commonly employed messages that focus on the importance of environmental protection are much less effective than a descriptive norm with a highly local geographical component.

Goldstein *et al.* call this type of proximate messaging a 'provincial norm' – capturing the fact that location is the foundation upon which the declaration is built. At first the provincial norm's success is slightly confusing, because there is no logical reason why behaviour in a room should be any more informative or diagnostic about normal social behaviour than the room across the hall, or on another floor. Indeed our behaviour often feeds off (and is a feeder of) our social, familial, and occupational groups, not the behaviour of strangers. However, with a little bit of investigation it is easy to find examples where the least personally meaningful but most proximate group are the dominant influencers of behaviour – supermarkets, libraries, cinemas, and traffic queues all come with clearly understood codes of conduct. This is so because it is an important social lubricant: 'If everyone knows the norms concerning a raised voice, or wearing bluejeans, then people can raise their voices, or wear bluejeans, without having to decide what these actions mean',[4] says Cass Sunstein.

Rather interesting for the commercial sector is this shot across the bows from Goldstein *et al.* about their towel reuse experiment: 'These findings highlight the utility of employing social science research and theory rather than business communicators' hunches, lay theories, or best guesses in crafting persuasive appeals.'[5]

When in Rome, do as they do in one particular upscale hotel in Phoenix, Arizona, or so it seems.

Stop! Start! Thief!

Describing what most people do worked very well for towel reuse. In fact, all the 'descriptive' norms worked well (gender, guest, etc.) even though the provincial norm won out. On the other side of the normative coin are the 'injunctive' norms. While descriptive norms are characterized as permissive behaviour that informs by example, injunctive norms are characterized by expectations of behaviour that curtail action.

Cialdini, Demaine, Sagarin, Barrett, Rhoads, and Winter tested the relative power of messages for Arizona's Petrified Forest National Park, which had just hit America's top ten most endangered list because of a massive theft problem.[6] The Petrified Forest regularly sheds small pocket-sized shards of wood millions of years old onto the floor. They are highly prized, and easy to pinch. The existing National Park signage – in attempt to reduce theft – described what was happening: 'Your heritage is being vandalized every day by theft losses of petrified wood of 14 tons a year, mostly a small piece at a time.'[7]

This is true. But not very helpful.

Arizona's Petrified Forest Rangers agreed to trial different signage designed by Cialdini *et al*. Trial paths were chosen, and the petrified-wood-strewn floor was decorated with extra secretly marked pieces of petrified wood. (They were pulled from the 'honesty pile' of stolen shards returned by guilt-ridden visitors.) Over two and half thousand visitors unwittingly walked the trial paths.

Without any sign on the trial paths, about 3% of the wood was stolen.

When signs were added, those that were negatively worded performed best in both the injunctive and descriptive conditions, so let's focus on those (a negative worded sign doesn't mean it's threatening or abusive – it simply describes behaviour in terms of what not to do – like the negative injunction 'Please don't leave your campfire' instead of the positive injunction 'Please stay with your campfire').[8]

In the negative injunctive condition the sign said, 'Please don't remove the petrified wood from the Park', and was accompanied by a picture of a lone visitor stealing a piece of wood, with a red circle-and-bar symbol superimposed over the hand. This instruction to 'not do something' is augmented by the image of the lone thief that says 'few people do this'. Which is true; few people do steal (even though it's a problem).

With this sign, less than 2% of the wood was stolen.

In the negative description condition the sign said, 'Many past visitors have removed petrified wood from the Park, changing the state of the Petrified Forest', and was accompanied by pictures of three visitors taking wood. This is also true – cumulatively, lots of people have stolen wood.

With this sign nearly 8% of the wood was stolen.

Quite clearly, for the Arizona Petrified Forest, 'a message that focuses recipients on the injunctive norm will be superior to messages that focus recipients on the descriptive norm',[9] and in fact the descriptive norm ('Many past visitors have removed . . .'), with its increase of theft to nearly 8% from the 3% no-sign test, is effectively a pro-theft message.

'Telling', instead of 'asking', is powerful.

However, the Forest Park administrators decided not to change their signs in line with the experimental results. Why? 'This decision was based on evidence from Park Ranger interviews with visitors, who felt that information indicating that the theft problem at the park was sizeable [as it was on the original sign] would not increase their likelihood of stealing wood, but would decrease it.'[10]

This is a terrible error.

They've fallen into the trap of asking people what they *think* is effective, rather than listening to the test data describing what *is* effective. If there is any lesson from this book, take that one.

What's even more galling is the understanding and implementation of behavioural initiatives is a battleground strewn with friendly fire. It's hard to get it right. It's hard to get it working without any unintended consequences. Indeed, as Stephen J. Dubner, co-author of *Freakonomics* and *Superfreakonomics*, says, 'A great many of these [behavioural psychology] initiatives will fail, for behaviour is harder to change than most smart people assume.'[11] I bet he didn't think the initiatives would fail, not because they weren't good enough, but because they'd be ignored.

In true negative injunctive tradition, *please don't remove psychological learnings from your messages.* (And I should include a pictogram depicting a lone respondent extracting psychology superimposed with a red circle-and-bar symbol stood separate from a group of others embracing learnings.)

Honesty is the best policy

The psychologist Michael Wenzel worked with the Centre for Tax System Integrity, Australian National University, to expand on some normative behaviour tests of his that examined misperceptions about tax compliance.[12]

It seemed that lots of Australians thought the average Australian was less honest than themselves on their tax returns. An oxymoronic condition, clearly, as only half of any set can be above or below the average. Wenzel and his team wanted to see if they could correct this assumption in a real-world situation.

They took a random sample of nearly 2,000 people and split them into four groups. They left one of the groups alone to represent normal taxpayers, and sent the same survey to the other three groups. (They didn't send it as-if from the taxman, to make sure people felt like they could be truthful.)

The survey asked about their own feelings towards earnings taxation and other deductions, as well as what they thought others' feelings were. One of the three remaining groups was left alone after that.

The other two were sent replies – one an injunctive reply clearly stating that whatever anyone thought, *in reality* most people are honest with their tax return. The other group was sent a descriptive reply stating that those surveyed said they were honest, but *they imagined* most other people weren't.

Of the four groups, the final two pitted an injunctive norm against a descriptive norm, similar to the Arizona Petrified Forest experiment.

Are the results similar?

It seems they are – the taxpayers who were informed that *in reality* normal social practice was honesty in tax returns reduced their average deduction claim from (Australian dollars) $286 to $151.[13]

The injunctive norm was successful in improving honesty in tax returns – but was it significant?

While the reduction in tax claims was almost exclusively drawn from the 'other deductions' section of the tax return rather than the main earnings or expenses part, this equates to approximately 5 million Australians making a claim. A crude projection of the $135 reduction onto these 5 million taxpayers sees total deduction claims reduced by $675,000,000.

That's quite significant.

The discrepancy between the average behaviour of people and the *perceived* behaviour of the average person can be pretty wide. And it seems in matters of taxation this discrepancy can be pretty valuable too.

Norms pervade behaviour so much that behaviour is often simply an expression of it. But norms are fragile – particularly when the discrepancy between public and private behaviour is large. In this case even small 'shocks' or observable changes in others' behaviour can lead to wholesale change; 'modest changes sometimes have a large signaling effect for other people . . . Something of this kind may have happened with respect to recycling' [14] in terms of its uptake, says Cass Sunstein.

The pervasiveness of norms has implications beyond cute signage and linguistic gymnastics. In terms of regulatory policy the legislariat tend to assume preferences are fixed, and as a consequence their calculations of the cost of change can be too high because they don't account for the possibility of observable changes in relatively few people catalysing a new norm that spreads effortlessly. By this same thinking, the cost to business of shifting normative behaviour in their favour can be less than they think, because they too assume a fixed preference unchanged by observable behaviour among their customers.

In terms of resource-stress reduction, the Climate Change Communication Advisory Group's (CCCAG) paper written by some of the country's leading psychologists involved in climate change issues for the UK government's Department of Energy and Climate Change (DECC), says: 'Where social norms can be combined with "intrinsic" motivations (e.g. a sense of social belonging), they are likely to be more effective and persistent.'[15]

Cass Sunstein, in his Law and Economics working paper, comments, 'changes in norms may be the cheapest and most effective way to make things better'.[16]

Well, when in Rome . . .

19 Make the question irrelevant

'Experience has shown . . . the larger portion of the truth arises from the seemingly irrelevant.'

Edgar Allen Poe

You can swerve all of our cognitive biases by placing the desired behaviour in lock-step with a situation that is unquestioned. Admittedly, it is a little 'Trojan Horse', although one of the largest and most successful 'make the question irrelevant' lock-ins has been around for nearly a century in Europe, and it has reduced electricity consumption for all of that time. I don't think I'll give too much away by saying it is an example of German efficiency at its best.

We'll come to that example last: It's not the only way to reduce stress on power production.

Lights. Out.

A lot of European hotels have keycard door locks rather than uniquely shaped metal keys. The keycards are the size and shape of a credit card and have a programmable magnetic strip. Partly because they don't look like keys, or behave like keys, it is challenging to stop them being misplaced. The financial cost to the hotels of misplaced keycards is minor compared to the cost of replacing uniquely shaped metal keys because the hotel simply programmes a new card for the customer rather than maintaining a stock of metal keys, but the 'cost' to the customer is annoyance and frustration.

They needed a keycard holder, preferably near the door.

Similarly, near the door in each room, hotels would post notices to remind customers to switch off lights and any other powered devices not needed while they were out.

The two problems combined to become one solution, in the form of a wall-mounted keycard holder and automatic power switch. When you took your key to leave the room all the power was switched off. On room entry, you put your keycard back in the slot on the wall-mounted holder and the power was restored.

This solution to the problem of how to ask customers to power down their room when they leave is not by clever signage, but by locking the action into the necessity of taking your key.

What's the benefit of this? A Berkeley Lawrence National Lab study by Erik Page and Michael Siminovitch monitored the electricity usage of hotel guests.[1] They found that bathroom lights were used for less than four minutes, but were frequently left on, giving an average on-duration of eight hours a day. That's quite a lot. Bedside lights had a similarly high on-duration: five hours. Most lights are low-intensity these days so the problems are mitigated by a technological solution, but air conditioning units don't share this benefit.

Unfortunately, where the keycard power-lockout has been adopted it is used as a total power shutdown, which can be a little overzealous for those who want to leave batteries on charge, or low-level temperature control on in excessively hot or cold climates. This is a criticism of the execution rather than the strategy.

Other executions of the lock-step approach include the designers of the UK's pedestrian crossings.

Of those crossings that have user-initiated traffic lights, the push-button device is fixed to the traffic light pole at waist height facing away from the direction of traffic. This forces the pedestrian to face the direction of the oncoming traffic when requesting to cross.[2] Neat. Similarly neat is the twist in cash machines – ATMs – where the cash is not dispensed until the card is pulled out. This sequence stops the old problem of people taking their cash and leaving their card behind.

This approach to behaviour – action rather than signage – makes the question irrelevant. It is familiar to product designers, part of the quiver of legislators, but largely ignored by marketers.

Kaiser chief?

Sunday, 30 April 1916 was a strange day for Germany. It was a day of adjustment and confusion in addition to the chronic terrors of the First World War.

That day of confusion started with Benjamin Franklin in the late 1700s. While the American envoy to France, he concluded that Parisians could save money on candles by getting up earlier to take advantage of morning daylight.

'Early rising' seems to be a theme of his, as he is often cited as the originator of the saying 'Early to bed and early to rise, makes a man healthy, wealthy, and wise.'[3] He certainly popularized this in his *Poor Richard's Almanack* (1733–58) – an almanac series that lasted twenty-five years – in October 1735, but the first English reference dates from 1496: 'As the olde englysshe prouverbe sayth in this wyse. Who soo woll ryse erly shall be holy helthy & zely.'[4]

Via Franklin's early rising, we jump to New Zealander George Hudson, who presented a paper in 1895 proposing shifting the clocks backwards and forwards.[5] Simply changing the clocks is a rather interesting solution to Franklin's candle-saving early-riser idea, although Hudson's reasoning was born of personal desire: as an amateur entomologist, he collected insects after working in an office during the day and so valued daylight greatly. There seemed to be something in the air: an English builder called William Willet also proposed a similar clock-changing solution. It was discussed in the UK parliament in 1908.[6]

But it wasn't until 1916 that the rubber hit the road. Germany wanted to conserve as much coal as possible for the war effort. At the time, incandescent lighting had a significant demand, so it made sense to minimize its use as much as possible, and that meant reducing the amount of domestic power needed. Was the solution a pleading sign? A demanding sign? An address from Kaiser Wilhelm II imploring subjects to ration lighting for the war?

None of those.

They passed a law to move the clocks forwards and backwards to take advantage of daylight. They were the first European nation to do so. Kaiser Wilhelm II nailed the solution by avoiding the question altogether. Most of Europe followed suit shortly after; Russia and the USA followed a year or so later.[7]

Today, the relationship between daylight-chasing and lower fuel bills is more complicated because residential energy consumption is drawn through many different devices, few of which relate directly to the amount of available sunlight. Similarly, life outside of the home is more complex than in 1916 with the leisure industry and farming communities disagreeing on the benefits of daylight-saving, among other interest groups.

But the fact remains; a swerve can avoid our cognitive biases by avoiding the question altogether.

Driving change

There must have been something in the water at the turn of the last century – 'swerves' were everywhere. Michelin wanted to increase profits made by their tyres. Which meant selling more. But they are not a commodity that one holds in stock like soup, or rice – you only need five tyres for a car. And they couldn't sell 'spares for your spares'. Also, they couldn't sell more cars (and hence more tyres) because they weren't a motor manufacturer.

All they could do was to get car drivers to wear their tyres out faster.

The solution? They made it chic to drive hundreds of miles by inventing the Michelin Guide. It contained everything you needed to know about staying, driving, and eating in Europe. All this done in (what was by today's standards) an uncomfortable car.

The Côte d'Azur had never seemed so sexy. Or close.

The answer on a plate

People who want to manage their calorie intake are often presented with a barrage of information. This is good, right? Because without information how can you make a considered choice? As we've seen throughout this book, information alone is not enough – in fact information alone is never 'alone'. It comes with a context, and that context will adjust our response.

Thinking laterally about context – even with calorific information and an overt desire to manage intake – will portion size covertly affect how much we eat?

Brian Wansink, James E. Painter, and Jill North pulled together fifty-four people of varying ages and body mass indices and split them into two groups. One group had a bowl of soup to eat. The other group also had a bowl of soup to eat, except it was a self-refilling bowl. The design incorporated a hidden tube at the bottom attached to a hidden larger bowl, so when they ate the level decreased more slowly than normal.[8]

How much do visual cues affect our portion judgment?

Those eating from the self-refilling bowl ate over 70% more. And if that wasn't odd enough: *they didn't think they had*. Gender made no difference, nor did their BMI. Everyone was 'fooled'. This type of visual portion cue isn't confined to the experimental laboratories – in 1970 the average diameter of a dinner plate in America was just 9 inches, and today it's over 30% larger.

A fact not lost on wayward ad man Alex Bogusky who wrote, in 2008, *The 9-Inch 'Diet': Exposing the Big Conspiracy in America*. The book convinces that there's a conspiracy to get us fat – not sure about that – but the central premise remains: visual cues affect our portion judgment.

If you're managing your calorie intake, use smaller plates: the food looks a lot bigger, and will satiate your hunger more efficiently.

And more importantly, you'll make the calorie counting questions irrelevant.

Outroduction

A long time ago, when my father was teaching me to drive, he was of immense help. He gave me a clear understanding of the mechanical process of driving, and took me for practice drives whenever he could. There's no substitute for practice, he said. The trick is to get to a point where the actions of driving are second nature so you can focus your concentration on the world outside your car.

Now you probably think this is going to lead into something about impulsive versus rational thinking. It's not.

When I passed my driving test – when I'd climbed that seemingly impossible mountain – I took my father out for a drive for the first time as a fully licensed driver. He said to me – just as we were about to pull away – now you've passed your test, *this* is when you really start to learn to drive.

And he was right.

Understanding how something works and being given the freedom to use it are only the beginning.

As you close this book, *this* is when you really start to learn to ask.

(Except of course if you read this bit before you got to the end.)

Glossary

I thought about a heavily technical glossary. I decided against it. There are plenty of papers, books, and indeed even entire libraries out there that'll explain each point in detail: there's little value in replicating that. (Sometimes, you have to take away options – see chapter 11.) So I've written a catchy bite-sized explanation – a 'pub' version, if you like. Dispensing with large tracts of dense explanation does mean a reduction in fidelity, so bear that in mind.

Altruism: Something that benefits another at the expense of the originator ('Let me get this'). If there's any expectation of return it then becomes reciprocal ('You get the next one').

Cost to the originator can be all sorts: time, money, calories, danger, etc.

See 'Reciprocation'

Anchoring: Recalled or recently realized information forms the basis for future decisions.

See 'Coherent arbitrariness'

Attraction effect/similarity effect: A new item in a group makes similar items attractive.

Authority effect: A statement made by a person who appears authoritative must be correct, because they look like they know what they're talking about. We fall prey because appearance is generally quite a good proxy for experience and knowledge. It's not always the case.

See 'Fundamental attribution error'

Bystander effect (Genovese syndrome): Someone else will do something about 'it'. And the more 'someone elses' there are, the longer it takes for someone to become the 'one' to do something about it.

Choice models, standard: Your 'best' choice is not affected by the number of inferior choices available. Disputed.

Coase theorem: The value of an object is independent of initial ownership – an assumption carrying great significance in the political economy. (And also second-hand car dealing.) Disputed.

See 'Endowment effect'

Cognitive dissonance: 'Your head says one thing, your heart says another.' Our gut reaction is at odds with our rational thought. Or, system 1 and system 2 are in conflict. (Avoidance is a common management strategy.)

Coherent arbitrariness: We start from a random point and then make non-random decisions based on that start point.

Commitment and consistency: If we publicly say we're going to do something we're more likely to stick to it (even if we feel the action is not right).

Confirmation bias: Something 'out of the ordinary' is considered as 'out of the ordinary', rather than considering the possibility that our understanding of 'what is ordinary' needs updating. Also, we tend to remember the past as a sequence of clear, composed events, rather than remembering the reality, which is a chaotic stream of events.

Construal level theory: *Where* in time you think about something affects *what* you think about it. The closer in time events are, the more we think about 'actions', and the further away events are the more we think 'in theory'. Happens in four dimensions. Can be in any combination:
  here/not here;
  me/not me;
  now/not now;
  definite/not definite.
  (In other words, 'can't see the wood for the trees'/'treetop view'.)

Context-dependent preferences: Your decision is affected by what's on offer – to the point where the addition or subtraction of things you *don't* want still affects your decision.

Correspondence bias: We think we know someone by what their actions tell us – even though their actions are forced by the situation they're in.

Decoy effect/asymmetric dominance effect: Similar things can often be compared, and graded. Take a group of houses that are better than others in some way – could be location, size, parking, garden – and if you add another house to the group that is itself dominated by one of the others on a/some points, you're more likely to choose the dominator.

Defaults: Nasty: They're not benign. They are usually considered to imply nothing – or at least are not considered important in their effect on choice (See 'Coase theorem') – but we infer huge amounts from them. Those who specify what is a default rarely know their power, and we that react to those defaults rarely realize how much we're affected by them: double whammy.

  They can imply ownership, which affects decisions. They can imply suggested preference, which brings out the authority effect. Anchoring, arbitrariness – the list goes on.

  See 'Anchoring', 'Authority effect', 'Coherent arbitrariness', 'Correspondence Bias', 'Endowment effect'

Duration-of-exposure: Increasing exposure to something un-owned increases attachment and valuation in a manner similar to actual ownership. Pre-auction browsing is a good example.

  See 'Endowment effect', 'Loss aversion'

Edge-aversion/aversion to extremes: 'Would you like a small, medium, or large coffee?' 'I'll have a medium, please.'

It's common to jump for the middle choice, and avoid the extreme dimensions: We rarely ask whether the 'medium' is 250 ml, like a small carton of juice? Or close to 330 ml, like a can of drink? Or about 500 ml – half a litre.

Suffice to say the middle choice is safe in many areas of life.

Endowment effect: Something owned is more valuable than something not owned: works for things 'outside your head' like products and the environment; works for things 'inside your head' like beliefs and defaults. Things inside your head can be twisted by the order in which they're asked (especially defaults). And things outside your head may be considered 'owned' before actual ownership takes place (like in an auction).

It may be the fear of loss that evokes endowment, rather than the pleasure of ownership.

Escalation of commitment: Investments should be made based on the future benefit – past investments are irrelevant. That's how it should be, but we tend to consider the past. It affects the outcome.

See 'Sunk-costs bias'

Familiarity principle: We like things because we are familiar with them. (Most of us want it to be the other way around: we're familiar with things because we like them.) The odd thing is, the effect can happen even in the absence of awareness.

See 'Mere exposure'

Finite pool of worry: The more things we worry about, the less capacity we have to worry about others, even when the 'others' haven't changed their likelihood of happening: 'When your bucket's full, your bucket's full.'

Framing: It's quite a broad term. In fact, almost all the other effects described here can 'frame' a choice, and in so doing create different outcomes. In that sense, 'framing' tells us that what is said is less significant than how it's said.

Fundamental attribution error: Someone's demeanor is explained by their personality rather than the situation they're in: talking to you while sitting in a dentist's waiting room will be different from talking to you while sitting in a hotel foyer on holiday.

See 'Authority effect' , 'Correspondence bias'

Goal Dilution: Broadly there are two things to remember with this – one about mental function and one about perception. In terms of mental function, if you have simultaneous inputs decision-making does not degrade gracefully; rather it's outsourced from your rational System 2 brain to your instinctive System 1 brain – the part that makes impulsive decisions. In terms of perception, something that has a lot of functions is seen as weak on all of them: a Jack-of-all-trades, master of none.

Habit: Type of behavioural lock-in where new information is not taken into account because conforming to habit delivers satisfying and direct personal outcomes. Persuasive messages aren't very persuasive on formed habits. Better to change the environment.

See 'Heuristics', 'Schema'

Heuristics: Similar to framing in the sense that it's quite a broad term. Heuristics are broadly the assumptions we make in order to understand and respond to the world without having to work everything out from the ground up: it delivers 'answers' for free. We might use a number of schemas to construct a heuristic. However, what we gain in speed of understanding, we lose in quality.

See 'Schema'

Jevons paradox (Jevons effect):   Production efficiencies will be used to increase output rather than increase downtime. (Efficiencies in golf ball manufacturing means more golf balls per worker, not more time off to play golf.)

Illusory superiority: The above-average bias – we all have it. We tend to overestimate our good points, and underestimate our bad points, in comparison to those around us. (Aren't we all better than average drivers?)

Inter-generational equity: Things of value that can be used to benefit the young, the old, or those who are yet to be born. Can be money, justice, the environment, or species diversity amongst other things.

Length of ownership: How long you've owned something makes you value it more – including items that you had owned in the past.

Loss aversion: We really don't like loss: We work harder to avoid it than we do to achieve gain. Any chance we have of gain is placed in the 'don't risk it' safe option mode, but to correct losses we seek risk and reward to 'get back to evens'. It's a 'non-return valve', if you like.

Mental accounting: Mentally, we store money in different ways: money yet to be earned (future pay rise, lottery win); money earned (wages, disposable income); money saved (useable savings, pension, house price). Future money has less spending friction than saved money.

(Mere) measurement effect: Being exposed to something, or giving your opinion on the same, lights up your attitude towards it. If that attitude is positive, you're more likely to conform to it later. (Habituation can weaken the effect.)

See 'Self-prophecy'

Messenger: A description that says we are heavily influenced by who communicates information – as defined by the Institute for Government think tank and the UK government Cabinet Office's. It's similar to the 'authority effect', if not the same.

See 'Authority effect'

Norms, descriptive: Shared understanding about expectations of behaviour commonly performed, as expressed (purposefully or otherwise) in some form (recognized or otherwise). Or, whether I know it or not, I will use other people's behaviour as my reference point so as not to appear the odd-ball

Norms, global: Universally shared understanding about expectations of behaviour in a group.

Or, generally speaking, if I behave in this way, no one will consider me the odd-ball.

Norms, injunctive: Shared understanding about expectations of behaviour commonly approved, as expressed (purposefully or otherwise) in some form (recognized or otherwise).

Or, whether I know it or not, if I behave like that I will not be considered the odd-ball.

Norms, prescriptive: Shared understanding about expectations of behaviour that are pervasive, 'unwritten', and almost unrecognized.

Or, I never realized that we all behaved in a similar way until that odd-ball arrived.

Norms, proscriptive: Shared understanding about expectations of behaviour that are pervasive, known, and cultural.

Or, I know that if I behave in this way, no one will consider me the odd-ball.

Norms, provincial: Shared understanding about expectations of behaviour in a particular place.

Or, if I behave in this way around here, no one will consider me the odd-ball.

Norms, social: Shared understanding about expectations of behaviour within a group. We tend to conform to expectations even though we like to think of ourselves as making personal and principled decisions. They are so pervasive it can be hard to spot, and vary from requiring tight conformity to allowing a wide variety of behaviour.

Or, if I behave in this way, no one will consider me the odd-ball (and no one wants to be considered the odd-ball).

Numéraire: The base unit of account. Usually money, but can be in the forms of goods (such as cigarettes in prison).

Output interference: When recalling information that we think relevant to a decision at hand, we can make links with other memories, giving them prominence, and reduce links with others that compete. But are those links useful? And are we recalling information that gives us the best possible outcome? If we are, it's by chance.

Placebo effect: In WWII a US Army nurse ran out of morphine. She injected a soldier with salty water instead, and told him it was morphine. It worked. The soldier felt minimal pain, and didn't suffer from shock.[1] (There are other less dramatic ways it can work.)

Pre-attentive processing: We experience the world through all our senses. It's filtered, so we can explore some of it further. It's the reason you hear your name called out in a busy room even though you're not following everyone's conversations. Things that *really* stand out don't need much processing so we get to them pretty quickly.

See 'Salience'

Price perception: We value something based on its price – we don't price something based on its value.

Primacy: The first things in a list are not often crowded out by other things, and are often better rehearsed, so better committed to long-term memory. (The rut has to start somewhere.)

Priming: The process of bringing to the forefront of our mind a particular understanding of the world immediately before or during a new situation: The smell of freshly baked bread or fresh coffee in a house for sale, for instance, brings to mind lazy Sundays at home – this 'home'?

Query theory: Says our preferences aren't worked out and stored for use at a later date ('My favourite colour is blue, my favourite food is sausages . . .'), but are constructed on-the-fly, based on the order in which we query information – and this shifts the focus of attention. There's some suggestion it can counter the 'endowment effect'.

If we misread the terms and think a package will arrive in 28 days but find out it's actually 14 days when we complete a purchase, we're delighted. If we misread the terms and think a package will arrive in 7 days but find out it's actually 14 days when we complete a purchase, we're infuriated. The order of information affected our opinion, even though they're both delivered on the same day.

See 'Endowment effect'

Recency: Recent information looms large because it is easier to recall from short-term memory than less recent information.

Reciprocation: We respond to positive actions with similarly positive actions, and we respond to negative actions with similarly negative ones. (Not altruism because that has no expectation of future response.)

See 'Altruism'

Refutational pre-emption: Person initially raises and directly refutes one or more specific challenges.

Salience: Contrast – the degree to which something 'stands out'. Doesn't so much depend on what it is, only that it's different from its surroundings: A bright yellow high-visibility tabard won't stand out in a room full of people wearing bright yellow high-visibility tabards. Interestingly, the more something 'stands out', the easier schemas associated with it are brought to mind.

See 'Schema'

Scarcity Value: Scarce items are considered more valuable than plentiful ones, irrespective of their actual value.

Schema: The abstract mental structure we use to understand the world. You can see children building them as they grow older: 'Look mummy, a horse; it has four legs, hooves, and fur.' 'That's a cow, dear.' (Prejudice is also an example of schema that prevents people from seeing the world as it really is and inhibits them from taking in new information.)

See also 'Heuristics

Self-prophecy effect: Positive or negative social norms define how you need to behave to be seen by others in the way you want. Once we've decided how we want to be seen, we tend to act accordingly.

Status quo bias: You don't like loss; you value higher that which you own: welcome to the status quo courtesy of loss aversion and the endowment effect. (Or, a bird in the hand is worth two in the bush.)

Substitution effect: If prices rise we buy less of something. Or we buy the same number of a less good version. However, our start-point and direction of change (more of lower quality, or less of higher quality) are considered neutral in economics. Query theory, endowment, anchoring, exposure, and defaults – they all tell us different.

Sunk-costs bias: Commitment to spending increases when losses also increase – the wild long-shot bet after losing on the dead certs. (Or, in for a penny, in for a pound.)

System 1 thinking: Our reactive, instinctive, rule-of-thumb 'brain': as fish swim in a shoal.

(The 'lower' or System 1 brain is impulsive, intuitive, associative, and rapid in its response. We often call it our 'gut' reaction. It is interested in immediate gratification – anything in the future is irrelevant, whether it's gratifying or displeasing. It is your petulant child stamping feet and demanding jelly and ice cream.)

System 2 thinking: Our calm, rational, calculating 'brain': as Bobby Fischer plays chess.

(We often spend time formulating rational reasons why we should take a course of action, when all we're doing is agreeing with our gut reaction.)

Temperature priming: Warm things are lovely, cold things are hateful. More than that, the temperature of something immediately prior or during an event colours your judgment in that regard.

See 'Priming'

Temporal discounting: We like immediate gains more than the promise of future gains, so the longer we have to wait for something, the less we value it.

Both your impulsive system 1 brain and your rational system 2 brain are interested in 'now', but system 1 always wins – future plans are only considered by your system 2 rational brain. It's why you set your alarm clock for a sensible time when you go to bed, but you hit snooze when it's time to get up.

Temporal distance: See 'Construal level theory'

Time inconsistency: The choices we make today about tomorrow are changed when 'tomorrow' comes – and variations there-in. It's another way of describing temporal discounting.

See 'Temporal discounting'

Tragedy of the Commons: It's a peculiar situation where a limited resource gives individuals benefit up to the point at which the resource collapses. At that point no one gets to benefit. It's a system that has no self-correction. This makes it a problem. The classic example is a fixed area of common grazing land used by livestock farmers – each farmer gets 100% of the benefit of adding a cow, but all the other farmers have to bear a share of the downside in the form of reduced grazing. This continues until there are so many cows that the grazing collapses and so is unable to support any cows for a long time. There are direct parallels with nuclear war (mutually assured destruction), safety helmets for professional ice hockey players, river water pollution, carbon dioxide emissions, and splitting the bill for a restaurant meal (each diner can enjoy 100% of the most expensive meal while only paying a percentage of the extra cost).

Public reputation can reduce the effect

WTA/Willingness to accept condition: How much you'll accept in compensation for letting go of something.

See 'Substitution effect'

WTP/Willingness to purchase condition: How much you'll pay for the privilege of acquiring something.

See 'Substitution effect'

Notes

Introduction

1 E. G. Ravenstein 'Italian explorations in the Upper Basin of the Jub', *Geographical Journal*, 3(2), (February 1894), 134–8.
David Turton, 'Exploration in the lower Omo valley of southwestern Ethiopia between 1890 and 1910'. revised version of a paper first published in Maria Caravaglios (ed.), *L'Africa ai tempi di Daniele Comboni*, Atti del Congresso Internazionale di Studi Africani, Istituto Italo-Africano e Missionari Comboniani, Rome, 19–21 November, 1981.
Luca Bianchedi, *Un destino africano. L'avventura di Vittorio Bottego.* Rome: Pagine, 2010.
2 University of Utah Public Relations (2005). 'The oldest *Homo sapiens*'. Press release, issued 16 February 2005, online www.eurekalert.org/pub_releases/2005-02/uou-toh021105.php (accessed Jan 2012).
Richard Leakey and his team of palaeontologists travelled in 1967 to the Kibish Formation along the Omo river in southernmost Ethiopia, near the town of Kibish.
3 *Ibid.*
4 William H. Calvin, *A Brief History of the Mind.* Oxford: Oxford University Press, 2004, chapter 9, online http://WilliamCalvin.com/BHM/ch9.htm (accessed January 2012).
5 Stephen Oppenheimer, 'Gate of Grief, 85000 years ago', Bradshaw Foundation, online, www.bradshawfoundation.com/journey/gates2.html (accessed January 2012).
6 Richard Gray (9 May 2009), 'African tribe populated rest of the world', *Daily Telegraph*, online www.telegraph.co.uk/science/science-news/5299351/African-tribe-populated-rest-of-the-world.html (accessed January 2012).
7 Anny Shaw (10 February 2010), 'Last member of 65,000-year-old tribe dies, taking one of world's earliest languages to the grave', *Daily Mail*, online www.dailymail.co.uk/sciencetech/article-1248754/Last-member-65-000-year-old-tribe-dies-taking-worlds-earliest-languages-grave.html (accessed January 2012).
8 Calvin, *A Brief History of the Mind*, online.
9 Matt Ridley (22 May 2010), 'Humans: why they triumphed', *Wall Street Journal*, online http://online.wsj.com/article/SB10001424052748703691804575254533386923138.html (accessed January 2012).
10 *Ibid.* online.
11 Mr Huggins (22 February 2002), 'Impact of the Railways', schoolhistory.co.uk, online, 2 (accessed January 2012).
12 *Ibid.* 3.

13 C. Nardinelli, 'Industrial Revolution and the standard of living', *The Concise Encyclopedia of Economics*, 2nd edition, online, www.econlib.org/library/Enc/IndustrialRevolutionandtheStandardofLiving.html (accessed January 2012).

14 W. Stephenson (6 September 2010), 'Can we expect to live to 77, 89 or 100?', BBC online, www.bbc.co.uk/news/magazine-11178319 (accessed January 2012).

15 Kaare Christensen, Gabriele Doblhammer, Roland Rau, and James W Vaupel, 'Ageing populations: the challenges ahead', *The Lancet*, 374 (9696), 3 October 2009, 1196-1208 (accessed January 2012).

16 A. Maddison, *Growth and Interaction in the World Economy: The Roots of Modernity*. Washington, CD:AEI Press, 2005, 5.

17 M. Ridley (30 June 2010), 'The Rational Optimist, by Matt Ridley: a book excerpt', Ode magazine, online, www.odemagazine.com/exchange/16888/the_rational_optimist_by_matt_ridley_a_book_excerpt (accessed January 2012).

18 M. Kirkpatrick (4 August 2010), 'Google CEO Schmidt: "People aren't ready for the technology revolution"', online, www.readwriteweb.com/archives/google_ceo_schmidt_people_arent_ready_for_the_tech.php (accessed January 2012).

19 S. Pinker, *The Blank Slate: The Modern Denial of Human Nature*. New York: Viking, 2002.

20 Daniel Kahneman and Amos Tversky, 'Prospect theory: an analysis of decision under risk', *Econometrica*, 47 (2), 1979, 263.

1 Just ask

1 This is a basic interpretation of quantum mechanics as described by classical physics (see the Copenhagen Theory). Today's understanding is more sophisticated but still contains the essential paradox that measurement/observation affects state (see Zeno's paradox/quantum Zeno effect).

2 M. Fishbein and I. Ajzen, *Belief, Attitude, Intention and Behavior: An Introduction to Theory and Research*. Reading, MA: Addison-Wesley, 1975, 369.

3 Vicki G. Morwitz and Gavan J. Fitzsimons, 'The Mere Measurement effect: why does measuring intentions change actual behavior?', *Journal of Consumer Psychology*, 14 (1–2), 2004, 64–73.

4 Anthony G. Greenwald, Catherine G. Carnot, Rebecca Beach, and Barbara Young, 'Increasing voting behavior by asking people if they expect to vote', *Journal of Applied Psychology*, 72, 1987, 315–18.

5 Morwitz and Fitzsimons, 'The Mere Measurement effect', 64–73.

6 G. J. Fitzsimons and D. R. Lehmann, 'Reactance to recommendations: when unsolicited advice yields contrary responses', *Marketing Science*, 23(1), 2004, 82–94.

7 Daniel Schneider, Alexander Tahk, and Jon A. Krosnick, 'Reconsidering the impact of behavior prediction questions on illegal drug use: the importance of using proper analytic methods', *Social Influence*, 2(3), 2007, 178–96.

8 D. Shaffer, A. Garland, V. Vieland, M. Underwood, and C. Busner, 'The impact of curriculum-based suicide prevention programs for teenagers', *Journal of the American Academy of Child and Adolescent Psychiatry*, 30(4), 1991, 588–96.

9 T. Mann, S. K. Nolen-Hoeksema, D. Burgard, K. Huang, A. Wright, and K. Hansen, 'Are two interventions worse than none?', *Health Psychology*, 16, 1997, 215–25.

10 U. M. Dholakia and V. G. Morwitz, 'The scope and persistence of mere measurement effects: evidence from a field study of customer satisfaction measurement', *Journal of Consumer Research*, 29, 2002, 159–67.

11 J. Levav and G. J. Fitzsimons, 'When questions change behavior: the role of ease of representation', *Psychological Science*, 17(3), 2006, 207–13.

12 *Ibid.* 209.

13 *Ibid.* 209.

14 *Ibid.* 210.

15 *Ibid.* 209.

16 *Ibid.* 209.
17 For more on this subject read Morwitz and Fitzsimons, 'The Mere Measurement effect', 64–73; Levav and Fitzsimons, 'When questions change behavior', 207–13.
18 Marlene B. Schwartz, 'The influence of a verbal prompt on school lunch fruit consumption: a pilot study', *International Journal of Behavioral Nutrition and Physical Activity*, 4(6), 2007.

2 Ask using the right words

1 David J. Hardisty, Eric J. Johnson, and Elke U. Weber, 'A dirty word or a dirty world? Attribute framing, political affiliation, and query theory', *Psychological Science*, 21(1), 2010, 86–92.
2 The money raised, they were told, would all be spent on tactics to lower the amount of carbon in the atmosphere – a simple closed-loop between monies raised and monies spent. This helps to negate the fact that, technically, tax money raised *can* be spent anywhere, but an offset can *only* be spent on an offset.
3 Published research contains a $345/$352 ticket price pair. Presentations available online by some authors of the research contain $392.70/$385.00 ticket price pair. Published values used where available.
4 The base price was a real price to keep it consistent with expectations, and the carbon cost was based on averaging existing carbon-offset providers' rates.
5 A. Tversky, (1996) 'Contrasting rational and psychological principles of choice', in R. J. Zeckhauser, R. K. Keeney, and J. K. Sebenius (eds.), *Wise Choices: Decisions, Games and Negotiations*. Boston: Harvard Business School Press, 5–21.
6 Hardisty, 'A dirty word or a dirty world?', 88.
7 Timothy K. M. Beatty, Laura Blow, Thomas F. Crossley, and Cormac O'Dea, 'Cash by any other name? Evidence on labelling from the UK Winter Fuel Payment', *IFS Working Paper*, 10/11, May 2011.
8 L. Goss, *The Art of Selling Intangibles*. New York: New York Institute of Finance, 1982, 150.
9 J. Godek and K. B. Murray, 'Effects of spikes in the price of gasoline on behavioral intentions: a mental accounting explanation', *Journal of Behavioral Decision Making*, first published online 22 March 2011.
10 G. Belsky and T. Gilovich, *Why Smart People Make Big Money Mistakes and How to Correct Them: Lessons from the New Science of Behavioral Economics*. New York: Simon & Schuster, 1999, 52.
11 N. Liberman, Y. Trope, and E. Stephan, 'Psychological distance', in A. W. Kruglanski and E. T. Higgins (eds.), *Social Psychology: Handbook of Basic Principles*. New York: Guilford Press, 2007, vol. 2, 353–83, atp. 362.
12 N. Liberman, Y. Trope, S. Macrae, and S. J. Sherman, 'The effect of level of construal on the temporal distance of activity enactment', *Journal of Experimental Social Psychology*, 43, 2007, 143–9.
13 S. Pahl, 'Psychological distance – exploring construal level theory in the context of sustainability', Seminar: Psychological Distance and Sustainability, 22 September 2010, School of Psychology, Cardiff University.
14 *Ibid.* 15.
15 Jonathon P. Schuldt, Sara H. Konrath, and Norbert Schwarz, ''Global warming' or 'climate change'? Whether the planet is warming depends on question wording', *Public Opinion Quarterly*, first published online 21 February 2011.
16 L. Whitmarsh, 'What's in a name? Commonalities and differences in public understanding of 'climate change' and 'global warming'', *Public Understanding of Science*, 18(4), 2009, 401–20.
17 Schuldt *et al.*, ''Global warming''.
18 Whitmarsh, 'What's in a name?'

19 W. W. (1 March 2011), 'Framing climate change', *The Economist*, online, www.economist.com/node/21016460 (accessed March 2011).
20 BBC (19 June 2010), *Electric Ride: Follow the Electric Car as It Crosses Europe*, online, www.bbc.co.uk/radio4/features/electric-ride/map/ (accessed June 2011).
21 Crispin Porter + Bogusky (2009), Marketing campaign website for Brammo electric motorbike company, online, www.shockingbarack.com (accessed July 2010).

3 Ask using the right images

 1 For more on Marstaller Inc. and its history: American Advertising Hall of Fame, Corporate website, online, www.advertisinghalloffame.org/members/member_bio_text.php?memid=704 (accessed March 2011).
    Genesis Burson-Marsteller, Corporate website, online, www.genesisbm.in/history.html (accessed March 2011).
    AdAge magazine (15 September 2003) Encyclopedia, Marsteller Inc., online, http://adage.com/article/adage-encyclopedia/marsteller/98763/ (accessed July 2011).
 2 *AdAge* magazine (15 September 2003) Encyclopedia, Marsteller Inc. online, http://adage.com/article/adage-encyclopedia/marsteller/98763/ (accessed July 2011).
 3 Robert B. Cialdini, Raymond R. Reno, and Carl A. Kallgren, 'A focus theory of normative conduct: recycling the concept of norms to reduce littering in public places', *Journal of Personality and Social Psychology*, 58(6), 1990, 1015–26.
 4 Robert B. Cialdini, 'Crafting normative messages to protect the environment', *Current Directions in Psychological Science*, 12(4), 2003, 105–9.
 5 *Ibid.* 99.
 6 DEFRA (2010) *Reflections*, Act on CO2 UK television advertising campaign, online, www.youtube.com/watch?v=yM01dRqjuhM (accessed July 2011).
 7 I. Ayres and B. Nalebuff (4 September 2006), *Easy Savings*, Forbes.com, online, www.forbes.com/forbes/2006/0904/146.html (accessed July 2011).
 8 M. Berners-Lee, *How Bad Are Bananas? The Carbon Footprint of Everything*. London: Profile Books, 2010, 18, 87 (calculation by O. G. Payne).
 9 Cialdini, 'Crafting normative messages'.
10 M. Phillips (2011), *The SOFII History Project: David Ogilvy's Letter for the United Negro College Fund, from 1968*, The Showcase of Fundraising Innovation and Inspiration, online, www.sofii.org/node/685 (accessed July 2011).
11 J. Goodhew, S. Pahl, and T. Auburn, (2011) 'Promoting energy efficiency in homes . . . by making heat visible through thermal imaging?', paper presented at Carbon Action Network conference 2011, Birmingham, Wednesday 25 May 2011.
12 *Ibid.* 21.
13 *Ibid.* 14.
14 *Ibid.* 19.
15 S. Darby, 'Communicating energy demand: measurement, display and the language of things', in L. Whitmarsh, S. O'Neill, and I. Lorenzoni, *Engaging the Public with Climate Change: Behaviour Change and Communication*. London: Earthscan, 2010.
16 B. Bollinger and K. Gillingham, 'Environmental preferences and peer effects in the diffusion of solar photovoltaic panels', Working paper: *Marketing Science*, August 2010.
17 N. Lessem and R. Vaughn, 'Image motivation in green consumption', Manuscript: UCLA Economics Department, 2009.
18 S. Simon (18 October 2010), 'The secret to turning consumers green. It isn't financial incentives. It isn't more information. It's guilt', *Wall Street Journal*, online, http://online.wsj.com/article/SB10001424052748704575304575296243891721972.html (accessed July 2011).
19 *Ibid.*

20 J. Farrell (5 April 2011), 'Solar is contagious', *Grist*, online, www.grist.org/solar-power/2011-04-05-solar-is-contagious (accessed July 2011).
21 Y. Trope, N. Liberman, and C. Wakslak, 'Construal levels and psychological distance: effects on representation, prediction, evaluation, and behavior', *Journal of Experimental Psychology,* 17(2), 2007, 83–95.
22 B. Horovitz (9 March 2010), 'Baby carrots take on junk food with hip marketing campaign', usatoday.com, online, www.usatoday.com/money/industries/food/2010-08-29-baby-carrots-marketing_N.htm (accessed July 2011).
23 E. Wu (5 January 2011), *Chopsticks for a Tree*, DDBChina Advertising agency website, online, www.ddbchina.com/ddblog/2011/01/chopsticks-for-a-tree.html (accessed July 2011).

4 Ask at the right time

1 Toyota Georgetown (2006–11), *History*, Toyota Motor Manufacturing, Kentucky, Inc., online, www.toyotageorgetown.com/history.asp (accessed June 2011).
2 Piggly Wiggly (29 September 2007), *Where It Began...*, Wayback machine: Piggly Wiggly Corp. Website, online, web.archive.org/web/20070929165051/http://www.pigglywiggly.com/cgi-bin/customize?aboutus.html (accessed June 2011).
3 B. Shiv and A. Fedorikhin, 'Heart & mind in conflict: the interplay of affect and cognition in consumer decision making', *Journal of Consumer Research*, 26, December 1999, 278–92
4 The 'Naughty . . . but nice' slogan was written in the 1970s for the National Dairy Council by the then humble advertising copywriter Salman Rushdie.
5 Shiv *et al*, 'Heart & mind in conflict', 290.
6 A. Smith, *An Inquiry into the Nature and Causes of the Wealth of Nations*, The Project Gutenberg EBook, 28 February 2009. www.theindependentpatriot.com/Liberty%20Reading%20Group%20Documents/1776_An_Inquiry_into_the_Nature_and_Causes_of_the_Wealth_of_Nations_by_Adam_Smith.pdf.
7 L. Mancino and J. Guthrie, 'When *nudging* in the lunch line might be a good thing', *Amber Waves*, 7(1), 2009, 32–8, www.ers.usda.gov/AmberWaves/March09/Features/LunchLine.htm.
8 Smith, *An Inquiry into the Nature*.
9 Information Display Company (8 June 2009), *New Traffic Flow Manager Works with Traffic Signal Timing to Eliminate Traffic Congestion and Reduce Fuel Consumption*, Corporate website: press release, online, www.informationdisplay.com/httpdocs/press_release_trafficflow_.php (accessed July 2010).
10 Information Display Company, *Intelligent Traffic Signs*, Corporate website, online, www.informationdisplay.com/httpdocs/idc-intelligent-traffic-signs.php (accessed July 2010).
11 *Ibid.*
12 Information Display Company (8 June 2009), *New Traffic Flow Manager.* **online,**
13 Sharecast (27 June 2011), *Carrefour Deal to Power Ocado Growth*, online, www.sharecast.com/cgi-bin/sharecast/story.cgi?story_id=4317567 (accessed July 2010).
14 H. Wilhite and R. Ling, 'Measured energy savings from a more informative energy bill', *Energy and Buildings*, 22(2),1995, 145–55.
15 S. Pahl, 'Psychological distance – exploring construal level theory in the context of sustainability', Seminar: Psychological Distance & Sustainability, 22 September 2010, School of Psychology, Cardiff University.
16 Cycling, however, isn't necessarily the panacea one might think. Although this book is not primarily about *what* to change rather than about *how to present* change in an attractive way, there are some interesting if rather fantastical crossover points between powered and unpowered transport. For instance, if you were able to get 100% of your calories for cycling from cheeseburgers your carbon dioxide emissions per mile would likely be about the same as two people driving

an efficient internal combustion engine car. (Berners-Lee, *How Bad Are Bananas*, p. 23.) I'm not sure how you'd do that, though. And Minetti and Gaspare from the University of Milan have found that hybrid cars can now trump at least one form of human locomotion – admittedly in a rather odd configuration: 'four men would release more CO_2 by jogging than if they boarded a hybrid car.' (A. Kuchment, 'When cars are greener than people', *Scientific American*, 22 April 2011, online, www.scientificamerican.com/article.cfm?id=when-cars-are-greener-than-people.)

17 L. Baker (16 October 2009), 'How to get more bicyclists on the road: to boost urban bicycling, figure out what women want', *Scientific American*, www.scientificamerican. com/article.cfm?id=getting-more-bicyclists-on-the-road (accessed July 2011).

18 *Ibid.*

19 *Ibid.*

20 *Ibid.*

21 Toyota Georgetown (2006–2011), *History*, Toyota Motor Manufacturing, Kentucky, Inc., online, www.toyotageorgetown.com/history.asp (accessed June 2011).

5 Ask with the right incentive

1 NPR (20 August 2010), *The Friday Podcast: Allowance, Taxes And Potty Training*, online, www.npr.org/blogs/money/2010/08/20/129328075/the-tuesday-podcast-allowance-economics (accessed July 2011).

2 *Ibid.*

3 K. S. Gallagher and E. Muehlegger, 'Giving green to get green? Incentives and consumer adoption of hybrid vehicle technology', Working Paper RWP08-009, John F. Kennedy School of Government, Harvard University, January 2008.

4 *Ibid.* 28.

5 Hoch *et al.* famously tested this by giving respondents the option of $10 now or $11 in a week. Most chose $10 now, even though the $11 is an inflation-busting 10% increase in a week. Our System 1 impulsive brain wins out over the rational System 2. For other respondents they changed the option but not the amount – $10 one year from now or $11 one year and one day from now. Most chose $11 one year and one day from now. Because both choices are now in the future, our impulsive System 1 is uninterested, so rational System 2 can work unimpeded, and chose the higher value.

Stephen J. Hoch and George F. Loewenstein, 'Time-inconsistent preferences and consumer self-control', *Journal of Consumer Research*, 17 March 1991, 492–507.

6 Gallagher and Muehlegger, 'Giving green to get green?', 28

7 *Ibid.* 29.

8 Renault, *Renault Z.E. (Zero Emission)*, Corporate website, online, www.renault-ze.com/en-ie/electric-motoring/renault-z.e.-in-detail/where-will-the-electric-cars-be-builty-2525.html&t=3 (accessed July 2011).

9 Volkswagen (2009), *The Fun Theory Campaign*, DDB Stockholm, online, www.thefuntheory.com/ (accessed July 2011).

10 Volkswagen (October 2009), *The Fun Theory Campaign*, Bottle Bank Arcade Machine, DDB Stockholm, online, www.thefuntheory.com/bottle-bank-arcade-machine (accessed July 2011).

11 Volkswagen (September 2009), *The Fun Theory Campaign*, The World's Deepest Bin, DDB Stockholm, online, www.thefuntheory.com/worlds-deepest-bin (accessed July 2011).

12 *Ibid.*

13 CNN.com (28 September 2005), *Talking Trash Cans Keep Berlin Clean*, CNN. com, online, http://edition.cnn.com/2005/TECH/09/27/spark.rubbish/index.html (accessed July 2011).

14 *Ibid.*

15 D. Kahneman and A. Tversky, 'Prospect theory: an analysis of decision under risk', *Econometrica*, 47(2), 1979, 263–92.
16 C. Jefferson (26 January 2011), *Idea: A Gym Membership that Charges You for Not Exercising*, Good Worldwide, LLC., online, www.good.is/post/idea-a-gym-membership-that-charges-you-for-not-exercising/ (accessed July 2011).
17 This is quite true financially, and is broadly true when the numéraire isn't financial, but does not describe all dimensions of construal – see Chapter 7, 'Ask for a commitment (in the future)' for more.
18 Volkswagen (December 2009), *The Fun Theory Campaign*, The Fun Theory award winner – The Speed Camera Lottery, DDB Stockholm, online, www.thefuntheory.com/2009/11/12/fun-theory-award-winner-speed-camera-lottery (accessed July 2011).
19 ParkHowell.com (13 June 2011), *'Speed Camera Lottery' Reflects the Spirit of Fun at Sustainable Brands 2011 Conference*, ParkHowell advertising agency, online, http://parkhowell.com/green-advertising-and-marketing/speed-camera-lottery-reflected-the-spirit-of-fun-at-sustainable-brands-2011-conference (accessed July 2011).
20 Gallagher and Muehlegger, 'Giving green to get green', 31.
21 Nudgeblog (9 June 2008), *Fayetteville's Energy Cop*, Nudgeblog.org, online, http://nudges.wordpress.com/2008/06/09/fayettevilles-energy-cop/ (accessed July 2011).
22 S. Penda (2 September 2003), *Congo's Football Officials 'Go Deaf'*, BBC News Brazzaville, online, http://news.bbc.co.uk/1/hi/world/africa/3201913.stm (accessed July 2011).

6 Ask – but have a default option

1 O. Morgans, *Stick or twist? An Analysis of Consumer Behaviour in the Personal Current Account Market*, Consumer Focus, October 2010, 4.
The divorce/bank switching statement is derived from the statement from Morgans' report that 'Three quarters of consumers (75 per cent) have never even considered switching their current account provider' and the fact that divorce rates in developed economies (such as the UK) are lower than 75%.
2 D. Pichert and K. V. Katsikopoulos, 'Green defaults: information presentation and pro-environmental behaviour', *Journal of Environmental Psychology*, 28(1), 2008, 63–73.
3 *Ibid.* 63–73.
4 *Ibid.* 69.
5 N. Welch (February 2010), 'A marketer's guide to behavioral economics', *McKinsey Quarterly*, online, www.mckinseyquarterly.com/A_marketers_guide_to_behavioral_economics_2536 (accessed July 2011).
6 Pichert, and Katsikopoulos, 'Green defaults', 69.
7 *Ibid.*
8 *Ibid.*
9 M. Gunther (17 November 2009), *When Behavioral Economics Meets Climate Change, Guess What's Coming for Dinner?* Greenbiz.com, online, www.greenbiz.com/blog/2009/11/17/when-behavioral-economics-meets-climate-change-guess-whats-coming-dinner (accessed July 2011).

7 Ask for a commitment (in the future)

1 J. Fuller, *Heads, You Die: Bad Decisions, Choice Architecture, and How to Mitigate Predictable Irrationality*, Per Capita Australia Limited, July 2009, 4.
2 For more on StickK: P. W. Grayson (5 February 2009), 'Dieting? Put your money where your fat is', *New York Times*, online, www.nytimes.com/2009/02/05/health/05iht-05fitness.19942435.html?pagewanted=all (accessed July 2011).

3 I. Ayres (17 September 2010), *Selling My Addiction*, StickK.com, online, www.stickk.com/articles.php?articleID=202 (accessed July 2011).

4 S. J. Dubner (30 May 2008), *How One Smoker Quit*, Freakonomics, online, www.freakonomics.com/2008/05/30/how-one-smoker-quit/ (accessed July 2011).

5 *Ibid.*

6 N. Liberman, Y. Trope, S. Macrae, and E. Stephan, 'The effect of level of construal on the temporal distance of activity enactment', *Journal of Experimental Social Psychology*, 43, 2007, 143–9.

7 Y. Trope, N. Liberman, and C. Wakslak, 'Construal levels and psychological distance: effects on representation, prediction, evaluation, and behavior', *Journal of Consumer Psychology*, 17(2), 2007, 83.

8 D. Leiser, O. H. Azar, and L. Hadar, 'Psychological construal of economic behaviour', *Journal of Economic Psychology*, 29, 2008, 762–76.

9 Trope *et al.*, 'Construal levels and psychological distance', 91.

10 *Ibid.* 85.

11 David J. Hardisty, Eric J. Johnson, and Elke U. Weber, 'Discounting future green: money versus the environment', *Journal of Experimental Psychology*, 138(3), 2009, 329–40.

12 N. Liberman, Y. Trope, and C. Wakslak, 'Construal level theory and consumer behavior', *Journal of Consumer Psychology*, 17(2), 2007, 113–17.

13 Trope *et al.*, 'Construal levels and psychological distance', 88.

14 M. D. Henderson, Y. Trope, and P. Carnevale, 'Negotiation from a near and distant time perspective', *Journal of Personality and Social Psychology*, 91(4), October 2006, 712–29.

15 R. Thaler, 'Some empirical evidence on dynamic inconsistency', *Economics Letters*, 8, 1981, 201–7.

16 Elke U. Weber, Eric J. Johnson, K. F. Milch, H. Chang, J. C. Brodscholl, and D. G. Goldstein, 'Asymmetric discounting in intertemporal choice', *Psychological Science*, 18, 2007, 516–23.

17 C. K. Hsee, R. P. Abelson, and P. Salovey, 'The relative weighting of position and velocity in satisfaction', *Psychological Science*, 2, 1991, 263–6.

18 G. Loewenstein and D. Prelec, 'Preferences for sequences of outcomes', *Psychological Review*, 100, 1993, 91–108.

19 Trope *et al.*, 'Construal levels and psychological distance', 90.

20 *Ibid.* 92.

21 'Dan Ariely on irrationality in the workplace' (February 2011), *McKinsey Quarterly*, online, www.mckinseyquarterly.com/Dan_Ariely_on_irrationality_in_the_workplace_2742 (accessed July 2011).

22 D. Read, G. Loewenstein, and S. Kalyanaraman, 'Mixing virtue and vice: combining the immediacy effect and the diversification heuristic', *Journal of Behaviorl Decision Making*, 12, 1999, 257–73.

23 D. McRaney (27 October 2010), *Procrastination, You Are Not So Smart*, You Are Not So Smart Blog, online, http://youarenotsosmart.com/2010/10/27/procrastination/ (accessed July 2011).

8 Ask in the right order

1 I. Ayres and B. Nalebuff (4 September 2006), *Easy Savings*, Forbes.com, online, www.forbes.com/forbes/2006/0904/146.html (accessed July 2011).

2 E. A. Morris, Cash for the Climate, 13 August 2009, www.freakonomics.com/2009/08/13/cash-for-the-climate/.

3 New York State Senate, Senator Squadron's Fuel Efficiency Bill Passes Environmental Conservation Committee, 3 February 2010, www.nysenate.gov/press-release/senator-squadron-s-fuel-efficiency-bill-passes-environmental-conservation-committee.

4 *Ibid.*
5 Ayres and Nalebuff, *Easy Savings*, online.
6 P. F. Drucker, *The Effective Executive*. London: Butterworth-Heinemann, 2007, 24.
7 B. B. Murdock Jr., 'The serial position effect of free recal', *Journal of Experimental Psychology*, 64, 1962, 482–8.
8 A. D. Smith, 'Output interference and organized recall from long-term memory', *Journal of Verbal Learning and Verbal Behaviour*, 10, 1971, 400–8.
9 S. Begly (27 February 2011), *I Can't Think!*, Newsweek Magazine, online, www. thedailybeast.com/newsweek/2011/02/27/i-can-t-think.html (accessed July 2011).
10 For more on memory see: G. D. A. Brown and S. Lewandowsky (2010), 'Forgetting in memory models: arguments against trace decay and consolidation failure', in S. Della Sala (ed.), *Forgetting*. Hove: Psychology Press, 2010, 49–75. David J. Hardisty, Eric J. Johnson, and Elke U. Weber, 'Discounting future green: money versus the environment', *Journal of Experimental Psychology*, 138(3), 2009, 329–40.
11 Begly, *I Can't Think!*, online.
12 F. Strack, L. L. Martin, and N. Schwarz, 'Priming and communication: the social determinants of information use in judgments of life satisfaction', *European Journal of Social Psychology*, 18, 1988, 429–42.
13 *Ibid.*
14 N. Schwarz, F. Strack, and H.-P. Mai, 'Assimilation and contrast effects in part-whole question sequences: a conversational logic analysis', *Public Opinion Quarterly*, 55(1) 1991, 3–23.
15 *Ibid.* 4.
16 *Ibid.* 25.
17 Hardisty *et al.*, 'A dirty word or a dirty world?'
18 *Ibid.*
19 *Ibid.*
20 S. Frederick, 'Cognitive reflection and decision making', *Journal of Economic Perspectives*, 19(4), 2005, 25–42.

9 Ask kinetically

1 P. Russo and B. Wypich (2 February 2009), 'Greener Gadgets | SmartSwitch | Peter Russo & Brendan Wypich, Stanford University 2009'. Bungalow, online, www.bungalow.ca/node/2009/02/greener-gadgets-smartswitch-peter-russo-brendan-wypich-stanford-university-2009/ (accessed July 2011).
2 F. G. Hamza-Lup, C. M. Bogdan, D. M. Popovici, and O. D. Costea (2011), 'A survey of visuo-haptic simulation in surgical training', paper presented at eLmL 2011, The Third International Conference on Mobile, Hybrid, and On-line Learning, Guadeloupe, France, 23–28 February 2011, 57.
3 A. Tonneau (2008), 'Interrupteur pulse', Alexandre Tonneau, online. www. alexandretonneau.com/pulse_switch.php (accessed July 2011).
4 J. Kestner, D. Leithinger, J. Jung, and M. Petersen (2009), 'Proverbial wallet: tangible interface for financial awareness', paper presented at TEI '09 Proceedings of the 3rd International Conference on Tangible and Embedded Interaction, 2009, 55–6.
5 J. Barth and R. Grasy (2011), 'DataBot Mouse', Interaction Design: HfG Schwäbisch Gmünd, online. http://vimeo.com/24741148 (accessed July 2011).
6 Traffic Advisory Leaflet 4/90, *Tactile Markings for Segregated Shared Use by Cyclists and Pedestrians*, The Department of Transport: Traffic Advisory Unit, 1990, 1-5.
7 F. K. Afukaar, 'Speed control in developing countries: issues, challenges and opportunities in reducing road traffic injuries', *Injury Control and Safety Promotion*, 10 (1–2), 2003, 77–81.

8 Cannes Lions Advertising Festival (2009), 'Melody Road', Cannes Lions Advertising Festival, online, www.youtube.com/watch?v=C-8AMlpzNwo&feature=player_embedded (accessed July 2011).

9 B. Johnson (13 November 2007), 'Japan's melody roads play music as you drive', *Guardian*, online www.guardian.co.uk/world/2007/nov/13/japan.gadgets (accessed July 2011).

10 S. K. Jensen and J. Freud-Magnus (1996), 'Asphaltophone', Gylling, Østjylland, Denmark, online, www.youtube.com/watch?v=ou-Xy5OI1kc (accessed July 2011).

11 C. Gibson (29 November 2007), 'Singing Streets and Melody Roads'. ABC News, online, http://abcnews.go.com/WN/Webcast/story?id=3931873&page=1 (accessed July 2011).

12 A. Piper (30 August 2010), 'Schadenfreude for the day: trucks running into a low bridge', 22 Words, online, http://twentytwowords.com/2010/08/30/schadenfreude-for-the-day-trucks-running-into-a-low-bridge/ (accessed July 2011).

13 Flickr (23 August 2009), 'If you hit this sign you will hit that bridge', Griffin, Georgia, US, online, www.flickr.com/photos/bgentry/3853508189/ (accessed July 2011).

14 Yale Bulletin (23 October 2008), 'With hot coffee, we see a warm heart, Yale Researchers find', Yale Office of Public Affairs & Communications, online, http://opac.yale.edu/news/article.aspx?id=6142 (accessed July 2011).

15 Y. Kang, L. Williams, M. Clark, J. Gray, and J. Bargh, 'Physical temperature effects on trust behavior: the role of insula', *Social Cognitive and Affective Neuroscience*, 6 (4), 2010, 507–15.

10 Add options

1 J. Huber, J. W. Payne, and C. Puto, 'Adding asymmetrically dominated alternatives: violations of regularity and the similarity hypothesis', *Journal of Consumer Research*, 9(1), 1982, 90–8.

2 J. Huber and C. Puto, 'Market boundaries and product choice: illustrating attraction and substitution effects', *Journal of Consumer Research: An Interdisciplinary Quarterly* (Chicago), 10(1), 1983, 31–44.

3 *Ibid.*

4 *Ibid.*

5 S. Vedantam (2 April 2007), 'The decoy effect, or how to win an election', *Washington Post*, online (accessed July 2011).

6 D. Ariely (1 July 2008), *Authors@Google*, online, www.youtube.com/watch?v=VZv-sm9XXU (accessed July 2011); www.youtube.com/user/AtGoogleTalks (accessed July 2011).

7 J. Huber, J. Payne, and C. Puto, 'Adding asymmetrically dominated alternatives: violations of regularity and the similarity hypothesis', *Journal of Consumer Research*, 9 (1), 1982, 96.

8 P. Dolan, M. Hallsworth, D. Halpern, D. King, and I. Vlaev (2 March 2010), *MINDSPACE: Influencing Behaviour through Public Policy*, The Institute for Government think tank & The UK government Cabinet Office, online, www.instituteforgovernment.org.uk/content/133/mindspace-influencing-behaviour-through-public-policy (accessed January 2011).

9 *Ibid.* 82.

10 Big Think (24 November 2009), *Dan Ariely: making money less abstract*, Big Think, online, http://bigthink.com/ideas/17458 (accessed July 2011).

11 *Ibid.*

12 W. Poundstone, *Priceless: The Myth of Fair Value (and How to Take Advantage of It)*. New York: Hill and Wang; first edn, 5 January 2010.

13 Vedantam (2 April 2007), 'The decoy effect, or how to win an election', online.

14 Yeo Sam Jo (15 June 2009), 'What rubbish', *The Straits Times* (Singapore), online, www.straitstimes.com/print/Singapore/Story/STIStory_390410.html (accessed June 2010).

15 Nudgeblog (September 2009), *The National University of Singapore nudges*, Nudgeblog, online, http://nudges.wordpress.com/2009/09/09/the-national-university-of-singapore-nudges/ (accessed June 2010).

16 N. Paumgarten (21 April 2008), 'Up and then down: the lives of elevators', *The New Yorker*, *online*, www.newyorker.com/reporting/2008/04/21/080421fa_fact_paumgarten?currentPage= (accessed June 2011).

17 M. Luo, (27 February 2004) 'For exercise in New York futility, push button', *The New York Times*, online, www.nytimes.com/2004/02/27/nyregion/for-exercise-in-new-york-futility-push-button.html?src=pm (accessed June 2011).

18 L. Cox (16 February 2011), 'London bike hire users can cut the scheme's carbon emissions', *Guardian*, online, www.guardian.co.uk/environment/bike-blog/2011/feb/16/london-bike-hire-emissions (accessed June 2011).

19 J. Huber, J. W. Payne, and C. Puto, 'Adding asymmetrically dominated alternatives: violations of regularity and the similarity hypothesis', *Journal of Consumer Research*, 9(1), 1982, 90.

20 Bike Europe (2011), *Market Reports United Kingdom 2010: Storming Year for the UK Bike Trade*, Bike Europe, online, www.bike-eu.com/facts-figures/market-reports/4919/united-kingdom-2010-storming-year-for-the-uk-bike-trade.html (accessed May 2011).

21 Pepsi Cola TV advert, (1973), Boase Massimi Pollitt, online, www.adslogans.co.uk/hof/IH002467.html.

11 Take away options

1 J. Surowiecki (23 July 2007), 'Fuel for thought', *The New Yorker*, online, www.newyorker.com/talk/financial/2007/07/23/070723ta_talk_surowiecki (accessed July 2011).

2 S. Duffy and M. Verges, 'It matters a hole lot: perceptual affordances of waste Ccontainers influence recycling compliance', *Environment and Behavior*, 41(5), 2009, 741–9 (first published online 14 October 2008).

3 @OctoberJones (24 January 2010), Twitter, online (accessed 24 January 2010).

4 Nudgeblog (September 2009), *The National University of Singapore nudges*, Nudgeblog, online, http://nudges.wordpress.com/2009/09/09/the-national-university-of-singapore-nudges/ (accessed June 2010).

5 Duffy and Verges, 'It matters a hole lot', pp. 744.

6 R. Glennerster and M. Kremer (March/April 2011), 'Small changes, big results: behavioral economics at work in poor countries', *Boston Review*, online, www.bostonreview.net/BR36.2/glennerster_kremer_behavioral_economics_global_development.php (accessed June 2011).

7 *Ibid.*

8 D. Ariely, *Predictably Irrational: The Hidden Forces that Shape Our Decisions*, London: HarperCollins; revised and expanded, 2009, pp. 111–17.

9 S. Iyengar and M. Lepper, 'When choice is demotivating: can one desire too much of a good thing?', *Journal of Personality and Social Psychology*, 79, 2000, 995–1006.

10 *Ibid.* 999.

11 S. Iyengar, W. Jiang, and G. Huberman, 'How much choice is too much? Contributions to 401(k) retirement plans', Pension Research Council Working Paper, October 2003.

12 S. Begley (27 February 2011), 'I can't think! The Twitterization of our culture has revolutionized our lives, but with an unintended consequence – our overloaded brains freeze when we have to make decisions', *Newsweek*, online, www.thedailybeast.com/newsweek/2011/02/27/i-can-t-think.html (accessed July 2011).

13 *Ibid.*
14 Iyengar and Lepper, 'When choice is demotivating', p. 996.
15 J. Hansen, S. Marx, and E. Weber, *The Role of Climate Perceptions, Expectations, and Forecasts in Farmer Decision Making: The Argentine Pampas And South Florida*, Final Report of an IRI Seed Grant Project, International Research Institute for Climate Prediction, 2004.
16 *Ibid.*
17 Ariely, *Predictably Irrational*,. 121.
18 John M. Darley and B. Latané, 'Bystander intervention in emergencies: diffusion of responsibility', *Journal of Personality and Social Psychology*, 8(4), 1968, 377–83.
19 Nobelprize.org (2005), *Thomas C. Schelling – Autobiography*, The Sveriges Riksbank Prize in Economic Sciences in Memory of Alfred Nobel 2005, online, http://nobelprize.org/nobel_prizes/economics/laureates/2005/schelling-autobio.html (accessed July 2011).
20 Surowiecki, 'Fuel for thought',online.
21 *Ibid.*
22 G. Hardin, 'The Tragedy of the Commons', *Science*, 162(3859), 13 December 1968, 1243–8.
23 *Ibid.*
24 Steven E. Landsburg (2009), *More Sex Is Safer Sex*, New York: Simon & Schuster, 6.
25 R. H. Thaler and C. R. Sunstein (6 April 2008), 'A gentle prod to go green: turning wishes into actions a matter of showing people the way', *Chicago Tribune*, online, www.chicagotribune.com/features/chi-nudging-polluters_thinkapr06,0,5299753.story (accessed July 2011).

12 Ask using the right authority

 1 S. Milgram, 'Behavioral study of obedience', *Journal of Abnormal and Social Psychology*, 67(4), 1963, 371–8.
 2 K. Wroth (15 December 2009), 'Vindication edition: Obama declares insulation "sexy"', *Grist* magazine, online, www.grist.org/article/2009-12-15-vindication-edition-obama-declares-insulation-sexy (accessed July 2010).
 3 TED Talks (18 February 2010), *David Cameron: The Next Age of Government*, Ted Talks, online, www.youtube.com/watch?v=3ELnyoso6vI#t=10m28s (accessed July 2010).
 4 C. Heath and D. Heath, *Made to Stick: Why Some Ideas Take Hold and Others Come Unstuck*. New York: Random House, 2007.
 5 @bobbyllew (29 June 2010), Twitter, online, twitter.com/#!/bobbyllew/statuses/17353003469 (accessed 29 June 2010).
 6 @EdwardNorton (27 January 2011), Twitter, online, twitter.com/#!/EdwardNorton/statuses/30428543431221248 (accessed 28 December 2011).
 7 M. T. Boykoff, 'Flogging a dead norm? Newspaper coverage of anthropogenic climate change in the United States and United Kingdom from 2003 to 2006', *Area*, 39(4), 2007, 470–81 (first published online 31 October 2007).
 8 P. T. Doran and M. Kendall Zimmerman, 'Examining the scientific consensus on climate change', *Eos, Transactions of the American Geophysical Union*, 90(3), 2009, 22.
 9 P. Downing and J. Ballantyne (2007) *Tipping Point or Turning Point? Social Marketing & Climate Change*, Ipsos MORI online, www.ipsos-mori.com/researchpublications/publications/publication.aspx?oItemId=1174 (accessed July 2011).
10 Trope *et al.*, 'Construal-level theory of psychological distance'.
11 S. Shackley and B. Wynne, 'Representing uncertainty in global climate change science and policy: boundary-ordering devices and authority', *Science Technology Human Values*, 21(3), July 1996, 275–302.

12 On 12 February 2002 the United States' Secretary of Defense Donald H. Rumsfeld told reporters in a Department of Defense news briefing: 'Reports that say that something hasn't happened are always interesting to me, because as we know, there are known knowns; there are things we know we know. We also know there are known unknowns; that is to say we know there are some things we do not know. But there are also unknown unknowns – the ones we don't know we don't know.'

13 P. Steele (11 July 2011), *You and Yours*, BBC Radio 4, online, www.bbc.co.uk/iplayer/episode/b012fbvy/You_and_Yours_11_07_2011/ (accessed July 2011).

14 V. Arroyo and B. L. Preston 'Change in the marketplace: business leadership and communication', in S. C. Moser and L. Dilling (eds.), *Creating a Climate for Change: Communicating Climate Change and Facilitating Social Change.*, Cambridge: Cambridge University Press, 2007, 319–38.

15 R. C. Anderson and R. White, *Business Lessons from a Radical Industrialist.* New York: St. Martin's Griffin, 2011, Foreword, xv.

16 D. Ratchford (September 2009), 'Smarter choices: Sutton's approach to behaviour change – and the work of the London Collaborative', *London Sustainability Exchange*, www.google.com/url?sa=t&source=web&cd=4&sqi=2&ved=0CBwQFjAD&url=http%3A%2F%2Fwww.lsx.org.uk%2Fdocs%2Fpage%2F3340%2FDaniel%2520Ratchford%2520-%2520lsx%2520presentation.pdf&rct=j&q=Daniel%20Ratchford%20Strategic%20Director%2C%20Environment%20%26%20Leisure%20%20B%26Q&ei=HEU0ToiCEsaChQfi6sWPCw&usg=AFQjCNGtYqXECNsJIqGL_ZWuzEfv2IRAXQ&cad=rja (accessed July 2010).

17 D. R. Abbasi, 'Americans and climate Change Closing the Gap Between science and action', *Yale School of Forestry and Environmental Studies*, 2005, . 63.

18 In the American State of Tennessee, the 1925 Butler Act prevented the teaching of Darwinian evolution in place of the biblical account. In that same year a biology teacher called John Scopes stood trial accused of violating the Butler Act because he taught Darwinian evolution in his biology class. The *State of Tennessee* v. *John Scopes* trial became a landmark American legal case, colloquially known as the 'Scopes Monkey Trial'.

19 J. M. Broder and K. Galbraith (8 October 2009), 'Defiant Chamber Chief Says "Bring 'Em On"', *New York Times* Green Blog, online, http://green.blogs.nytimes.com/2009/10/08/defiant-chamber-chief-says-bring-em-on/# (accessed July 2011).

20 Acclimatise, IBM (2009), *Carbon Disclosure Project Report, Global Oil and Gas, Building Business Resilience to Inevitable Climate*, IBM Corporate website, online, www-5.ibm.com/uk/green/cdp2009/oil_and_gas.pdf (accessed July 2011).

21 *Ibid*. 21.

22 M. Cote (29 March 2011), *They Know but Won't Admit: How Oil and Gas Companies Are Adapting to Climate Change*, Good Worldwide, LLC, online, www.good.is/post/they-know-but-won-t-admit-how-oil-and-gas-companies-are-adapting-to-climate-change/ (accessed July 2011).

23 S. C. Moser and L. Dilling, 'Communicating climate change: opportunities and challenges for closing the science-action gap', in J. S. Dryzek, Richard B. Norgaard, and David Schlosberg (eds.), *The Oxford Handbook of Climate Change and Society*, Oxford: Oxford Unitversity Press, 2011,167.

24 M. Gladwell, *The Tipping Point: How Little Things Can Make a Big Difference*, London: Abacus, 2001.

25 Consumerology (24 July 2009), *Overcoming Vanity with Hypocrisy*, Consumerology, online, www.consumerology.com/blog/post/overcoming-vanity-with-hypocrisy/ (accessed July 2011).

26 K. Kettle and G. Häubl, 'The signature effect: how signing one's name influences consumption-related behavior', *Journal of Consumer Research* (forthcoming).

27 *Ibid*. 8.

28 *Ibid.* 39.
29 *Ibid.* 39.
30 R. L. Zweigenhaft, 'The empirical study of signature size', *Social Behavior and Personality*, 5(1), 1977, 177–85.
31 S. Martin (March 2011), *What Is the Hidden Influence of Signing Your Name? The 'Signature Effect'*, Inside Influence Report, online, www.insideinfluence.com/inside-influence-report/2011/03/what-is-the-hidden-influence-of-signing-your-name-the-signature-effect.html (accessed July 2011).
32 BBC News (19 March 2009), *Store Owner Takes on Litterbugs*, BBC News, online, http://news.bbc.co.uk/1/hi/england/gloucestershire/7952397.stm (accessed July 2011).
33 BBC News (3 August 2005), *Bank Sorry for 'Insult' Cash Card*, BBC News, online, http://news.bbc.co.uk/1/hi/england/essex/4741017.stm (accessed July 2011).

13 Ask using the right *fake* authority

1 Humanoid Robotics Group, *Kismet,* MIT Artificial Intelligence Laboratory, online, www.ai.mit.edu/projects/humanoid-robotics-group/kismet/kismet.html (accessed July 2011).
2 V. Woods (18 March 2005), 'Pay up, you are being watched', *New Scientist*, online, www.vanessawoods.net/pdf/kismet.pdf (accessed July 2011).
3 *Ibid.*
4 M. Bateson, D. Nettle, and G. Roberts, 'Cues of being watched enhance cooperation in a real-world setting', *Biology Letters*, 2(3), 2003, 412–14, www.ncbi.nlm.nih.gov/pmc/articles/PMC1686213/.
5 D. Mackenzie (28 June 2006), '"Big Brother" eyes make us act more honestly', *New Scientist*, online, www.newscientist.com/article/dn9424-big-brother-eyes-make-us-act-more-honestly.html (accessed July 2011).
6 *Ibid.*
7 Bateson *et al.*, 'Cues of being watched', 412–14.
8 M. Milinski, D. Semmann, and H.-J. Krambeck, 'Reputation helps solve the "tragedy of the commons"', *Nature*, 415 (2002), 424–6.
9 South Lanarkshire Council County Council (October 2007), *Speed signs Reduce You to a Smile*, South Lanarkshire Council County Council, online, www.southlanarkshire.gov.uk/portal/page/portal/EXTERNAL_WEBSITE_DEVELOPMENT/SLC_ONLINE_HOME/SLC_NEWS/NEWS_STORY?content_id=13744 (accessed 2009).
10 *Ibid.*
11 O. Svenson, 'Are we all less risky and more skillful than our fellow drivers?', *Acta Psychologica*, V47(2), 1981, 143–8.
12 C. E. Preston and S. Harris, 'Psychology of drivers in traffic accidents', *Journal of Applied Psychology*, 49(4), 1965, 284–8.
13 D. Lovallo and O. Sibony (March 2010), 'The case for behavioral strategy', *McKinsey Quarterly*, online, www.mckinseyquarterly.com/The_case_for_behavioral_strategy_2551 (accessed July 2011).
14 Office of the Press Secretary (5 March 2010), *Remarks by the President on Clean Energy Jobs*, The White House, online, www.whitehouse.gov/the-press-office/remarks-president-clean-energy-jobs (accessed July 2011).
15 D. A. Fahrenthold (8 December 2009), 'Climate change is latest problem that's admitted but ignored', *Washington Post*, online, www.washingtonpost.com/wp-dyn/content/article/2009/12/04/AR2009120403619_2.html (accessed July 2011).
16 P. W. Schultz, J. M. Nolan, R. B. Cialdini, N. J. Goldstein, and V. Griskevicius, 'Constructive, destructive, and reconstructive power of social norms', *Psychological Science*, 18(5), May 2007, 429–34.
17 Opower, *Results*, Opower.com corporate website, online, http://opower.com/uploads/result/image/1/1.png?1308155443 (accessed July 2011).

18 Office of the Press Secretary, *Remarks by the President*, online.
19 R. Fisman (23 April 2010), 'Nudges gone wrong: a program designed to reduce energy consumption persuaded some Republicans to consume more', *Slate*, online, www.slate.com/id/2251658/#D (accessed July 2011).
20 W. S. Jevons, *The Coal Question: An Enquiry Concerning the Progress of the Nation, and the Probable Exhaustion of Our Coal-mines*, Google books, 1865. http://books.google.com/books?id=gAAKAAAAIAAJ&printsec=frontcover&source=gbs_ge_summary_r&cad=0#v=onepage&q&f=false (accessed July 2011).
21 Woods, 'Pay up, you are being watched', online

14 Let the feedback ask the question

1 M. Best, D. Neuhauser, and W. A. Shewhart, 'Walter A Shewhart, 1924, and the Hawthorne factory', *Quality and Safety in Health Care*, 15(2), 2006, 142–3. www.ncbi.nlm.nih.gov/pmc/articles/PMC2464836/ (accessed July 2011).
2 Henry A. Landsberger, *Hawthorne Revisited*, Ithaca, NY: Cornell University, 1958.
3 B. Goldacre, *Bad Science*, London: Fourth Estate, 2009, 139.
4 Best *et al.*, 'Walter A Shewhart, 1924, and the Hawthorne factory', online.
5 Ambient Devices, Inc., *Science*, Ambient Devices, Inc., online, www.ambientdevices.com/cat/science.html (accessed July 2011).
6 S. Seri, F. Pisani, J. N. Thai, and A. Cerquiglini, 'Pre-attentive auditory sensory processing in autistic spectrum disorder. Are electromagnetic measurements telling us a coherent story?', *International Journal of Psychophysiology*, 63(2), 2007, 159–63. A. Tales, J. Haworth, G. Wilcock, P. Newton, and S. Butler, 'Visual mismatch negativity highlights abnormal pre-attentive visual processing in mild cognitive impairment and Alzheimer's disease', *Neuropsychologia*, 46(5), 2008, 1224–32.
7 *The Economist* (10 June 2004), 'Background illumination', *Technology Quarterly*, online, www.economist.com/node/2724516?story_id=2724516 (accessed July 2011).
8 C. Thompson (24 July 2007), 'Clive Thompson thinks: desktop orb could reform energy hogs', *Wired* magazine: issue 15.08, online, www.wired.com/techbiz/people/magazine/15-08/st_thompson (accessed July 2011).
9 *Ibid.*
10 @Gibbzer (2010), *Twitter*, Twitter.com, online, twitter.com/#!/gibbzer (accessed 11 January 2011).
11 *Ibid.* twitter.com/#!/gibbzer/status/24829713750958080.
12 *Ibid.* twitter.com/#!/gibbzer/status/24832340895207424.
13 *Ibid.* twitter.com/#!/gibbzer/status/24832905251397632.
14 *Ibid.* twitter.com/#!/gibbzer/status/24833266582290432.
15 *Ibid.* twitter.com/#!/gibbzer/status/24834065911783425.
16 J. H. van Houwelingen and W. F. van Raaij, 'The effect of goal-setting and daily electronic feedback on in-home energy use', *Journal of Consumer Research*, 16, 1989, 98–105.
17 S. Darby, 'The effectiveness of feedback on energy consumption', *Review for DEFRA of the Literature on Metering, Billing and Direct Displays*, April 2006, 12.
18 *Ibid.* 13.
19 *Ibid.* 15.
20 W. Kempton and L. L. Layne, 'The consumer's energy analysis environment', *Energy Policy, Elsevier*, 22(10), 1994, 857–66.
21 S. Lacy (22 February 2010), *Al Gore Joins Richard Branson in Backing GreenRoad*, Techcrunch.com, online, techcrunch.com/2010/02/22/al-gore-joins-richard-branson-in-backing-greenroad/ (accessed July 2011).
22 M. S. Rosenwald (26 May 2008), 'For hybrid drivers, every trip is a race for fuel efficiency', *Washington Post*, www.washingtonpost.com/wp-dyn/content/article/2008/05/25/AR2008052502764.html (accessed July 2011).

23 *Ibid.* 2.
24 S. Deterding (24 September 2010), *Pawned: Gamification and Its Discontents*, Playful 2010, London, online, www.slideshare.net/dings/pawned-gamification-and-its-discontents/40 (accessed July 2011).
25 A. Jha (29 September 2008), 'Mobile phones to track carbon footprint', *Guardian*, online, www.guardian.co.uk/environment/2008/sep/29/carbonfootprints.traveland transport (accessed July 2011).
26 'Coined by Robert Metcalfe, founder of networking equipment company 3Com, Metcalfe's law says that the usefulness of a network equals the square of the number of users.' S. London, Financial Times lexicon, FT.com, online lexicon. ft.com/Term?term=Metcalfe%27s-law (accessed Nov 2011).

15 Ask nothing – other than to go public

1 J. Hammacott, 'Ignaz Semmelweiss: saviour of mothers', *Catalyst: Secondary Science Review*, 20(1), 2009, 4–5.
2 *Ibid.* 5.
3 J. Goldstien (25 November 2009), *How Undergrads Make Doctors Wash Their Hands*, Wall Street Journal Blog, online, http://blogs.wsj.com/health/2009/11/25/how-undergrads-make-doctors-wash-their-hands/?utm_source=feedburner&utm_medium=feed&utm_campaign=Feed%3A+wsj%2Fhealth%2Ffeed+%28WSJ.com%3A+Health+Blog%29&utm_content=Bloglines (accessed July 2011).
4 T. Rosenthal, M. Erbeznik, T. Padilla, T. Zaroda, D. H. Nguyen, and M. Rodriguez, 'Observation and measurement of hand hygiene and patient identification improve compliance with patient safety practices', *Academic Medicine*, 84(12), 2009, 1705–12.
5 *Ibid.* 1705.
6 T. Rendón, 'Using personalized normative feedback to reduce alcohol consumption: a cross-cultural comparison', Master's thesis, California State University, Committee Chair, 2008.
7 Yale Law School (30 August 2002), *Prof. Dan Esty Receives ABA Award for Achievement in Environmental Law and Policy*, Yale Law School, online, www.law.yale.edu/news/4346.htm (accessed July 2011).
8 I. Ayres and B. Nalebuff (4 September 2006), *Easy Savings*, Forbes.com, online, www.forbes.com/forbes/2006/0904/146.html (accessed July 2011).
9 R. H. Thaler and C. R. Sunstein (6 April 2008), 'A gentle prod to go green: turning wishes into actions a matter of showing people the way', *Chicago Tribune*, online, www.chicagotribune.com/features/chi-nudging-polluters_thinkapr06,0,5299753.story (accessed July 2011).
10 EPA press release (3 October 1990), *1988 Toxic Release Inventory National Report Available*, United States Environmental Protection Agency, online, www.epa.gov/history/org/tri/02.html (accessed July 2011).
11 S. M. Wolf, 'Fear and loathing about the public right to know: the surprising success of the Emergency Planning and Community Right-to-Know Act', *Journal of Land Use and Environmental Law*, 11(2), 1996, 217–325.
12 *Ibid.* 283.
13 *Ibid.* 282.
14 *Ibid.* 309.
15 G. C. Unruh (22 March 2010), *Can You Compete on Sustainability?*, Harvard Blog Network, Havard Business Review, online, http://blogs.hbr.org/cs/2010/03/can_you_compete_on_sustainabil.html (accessed July 2011).
16 D. D. Guzman (2 March 2010), *Walmart's Supply Chain Beware*, theenergycollective, online, http://theenergycollective.com/dorisdeguzman/32303/walmarts-supply-chain-beware (accessed July 2011).

17 M. Gunther (22 October 2009). *FedEx: Pushing the Envelope on Sustainability*, theenergycollective, online, http://theenergycollective.com/marcgunther/28372/fedex-pushing-envelope-sustainability (accessed July 2011).

18 Unruh, *Can You Compete on Sustainability?*, online.

19 Environmental Defense Fund (2010), *Poland Spring Reduces Idling to Curb Emissions*, Environmental Defense Fund, online, http://business.edf.org/casestudies/poland-spring-reduces-idling-curb-emissions (accessed July 2011).

20 *Ibid.*

21 *Ibid.*

22 F. W. Siero, A. B. Bakker, G. B. Dekker, and M. T. C. Van Den Burg, 'Changing organizational energy consumption behavior through comparative feedback', *Journal of Environmental Psychology*, 16, 1996, 235–46.

23 *Ibid.* 235.

24 *Ibid* 235.

25 G. Z. Jin, and P. Leslie, 'The effect of information on product quality: evidence from restaurant hygiene grade cards', *Quarterly Journal of Economics*, 118, 2003, 409–51.

26 *Ibid.* 438.

16 Ask for it back

1 David Ogilvy says: 'You aren't advertising to a standing army; you are advertising to a moving parade.' For more see D. Ogilvy, *Ogilvy on Advertising*. New York:Vintage Books, first edn 1985, 21.

2 N. Welch (February 2010), 'A marketer's guide to behavioral economics', *McKinsey Quarterly*, online, www.mckinseyquarterly.com/A_marketers_guide_to_behavioral_economics_2536 (accessed July 2011).

3 *Ibid.*

4 Pichert and Katsikopoulos, 'Green defaults'.

5 *Ibid.* 70.

6 R. B. Boyce, T. C. Brown, G. H. McClelland, G. L. Peterson, and W. D. Schulze, 'An experimental examination of intrinsic values as a source of the WTA-WTP disparity', *American Economic Review*,82(5), 1992, 1366–73.

7 C. R. Sunstein, 'Endogenous preferences, environmental law', John M. Olin Law & Economics Working Paper No. 14 (2nd series), 12.

8 *Ibid.* p. 12.

9 *Ibid.* 13.

10 *Ibid.* 13.

11 D. R. Abbasi, *Americans and Climate Change Closing the Gap Between Science and Action*, A Synthesis of Insights and Recommendations from the 2005 Yale F&ES Conference on Climate Change, Yale Project on Climate Change Communication, 2005, p. 101.

12 D. Kahneman, J. L. Knetsch, and R. H. Thaler, 'Anomalies: the endowment effect, loss aversion, and status quo bias', *Journal of Economic Perspectives*, 5(1), 1991, 193–206.

13 *Ibid.* 196.

14 S. F. Brosnan, O. D. Jones, S. P. Lambeth, M. C. Mareno, A. S. Richardson, and S. Schapiro, 'Endowment effects in chimpanzees', *Current Biology*, 17, 2007, 1704–7.

15 *Ibid.* 1705.

16 *Ibid.* 1705.

17 *Ibid.* 1704.

18 *Ibid.* 1706.

19 F. Bruni (18 August 2009), 'What they brought to the table', *New York Times*, online,www.nytimes.com/2009/08/19/dining/19note.html?pagewanted=2&8dpc&_r=2 (accessed July 2011).

20 *Ibid.*

21 E. J. Johnson, G. Häubl, and A. Keinan, 'Aspects of endowment: a query theory of value construction', *Journal of Experimental Psychology: Learning, Memory, and Cognition*, 33(3), 2007, 461–74.
22 H. Shefrin and M. Statman, 'The disposition to sell winners too early and ride losers too long: theory and evidence', *Journal of Finance, American Finance Association*, 40(3), 1985, 777–90.
23 T. Blair, *A Journey*, New York: Random House, 2010, 256.
24 Sunstein, 'Endogenous preferences, environmental law', 10.
25 J. R. Wolf, H. R. Arkes, and W. A. Muhanna, 'The power of touch: an examination of the effect of duration of physical contact on the valuation of objects', *Judgment and Decision Making*, 3(6), 2008, 476–82.
26 *Ibid*. 481.
27 *Ibid*. 481.
28 Nissan LEAF, Nissan LEAF promotional website, online, http://nissan.externaldatas.com/nissannewcastle/ (accessed July 2011).
29 Pichert and Katsikopoulos, 'Green defaults', 70.
30 Elke U. Weber, Eric J. Johnson, K. F. Milch, H. Chang, J. C. Brodscholl, and D. G. Goldstein, 'Asymmetric discounting in intertemporal choice', *Psychological Science*, 18, 2007, 516–23.
31 Johnson *et al.*, 'Aspects of endowment', 462.
32 S. J. Hoch, 'Availability and interference in predictive judgment', *Journal of Experimental Psychology, Learning, Memory, and Cognition*, 10, 1984, 649–62.
33 Wolf *et al.*, 'The power of touch', 476.
34 Kahneman *et al.*, 'Anomalies', 197.

17 Ask a different question

1 M. Mengisen (16 October 2009), *FREAK Shots: Nudging the Calorie Counters*, Freakonomics Blog, online, www.freakonomics.com/2009/10/16/freak-shots-nudging-the-calorie-counters/ (accessed July 2011).
2 L. Hickman (23 September 2010), 'What psychology can teach us about our response to climate change', *Guardian*, online, www.guardian.co.uk/environment/blog/2010/sep/23/climate-change-psychology-response-scepticism (accessed May 2011).
3 S. Clifford (1 March 2008), 'How fast can this thing go, anyway?', *Inc. Magazine*, online, www.inc.com/magazine/20080301/how-fast-can-this-thing-go-anyway.html (accessed June 2011).
4 Zipcar, *Green Benefits*, Zipcar corporate website, online, www.zipcar.com/is-it/greenbenefits (accessed June 2011).
5 M. Wall and E. Chipperfield (25 April 2010), 'WhipCar: I'm the girl next door, fancy hiring my car?', *Sunday Times*, online, www.timesonline.co.uk/tol/driving/features/article7105718.ece (accessed June 2011).
6 K. Belson (16 December 2008), 'Hertz tosses some car keys into the ring, battling Zipcar', *New York Times*, online, www.nytimes.com/2008/12/17/business/17hertz.html (accessed June 2011).
7 S. A. Shaheen and E. Martin, *Assessing Early Market Potential for Carsharing in China: A Case Study of Beijing*, Institute of Transportation Studies, University of California, Davis, 2006.
8 Relaxnews (13 May 2011) 'Volkswagen becomes latest automaker to enter car-sharing business', *Independent* newspaper, online, www.independent.co.uk/life-style/motoring/volkswagen-becomes-latest-automaker-to-enter-carsharing-business-2283656.html (accessed June 2011).
9 *Ibid*.
10 Trope *et al.*, 'Construal-level theory of psychological distance'.
11 M. Lane (3 March 2011), 'How warm is your home?', BBC News Magazine, online, www.bbc.co.uk/news/magazine-12606943 (accessed June 2011).

12 K. C. Arabe (11 April 2003), *'Dummy' Thermostats Cool Down Tempers, Not Temperatures*, ThomasNet News, online, http://news.thomasnet.com/IMT/archives/2003/04/dummy_thermosta.html (accessed June 2011).
13 M. Schäfer and S. Bamberg, 'Breaking habits: linking sustainable consumption campaigns to sensitive events', Proceedings of the 2008 SCORE Conference 'Sustainable Consumption and Production: Framework for Action', 10–11 March 2008, Brussels, Belgium, 213–28.
14 K. Maréchal, 'An evolutionary perspective on the economics of energy consumption: the crucial role of habits', *Journal of Economic Issues*, 43(1), 2009, 69–88.
15 *Ibid.* 81.
16 M. Martiskaïnen, 'Household energy consumption and behavioural change – the UK perspective', Proceedings of the SCORE 2008 Conference 'Sustainable Consumption and Production: Framework for Action', 10–11 March 2008, Brussels, Belgium, 73–90.
17 J. A. Bargh 'The Four Horsemen of automaticity: awareness, efficiency, intention, and control in social cognition', in R. S. Wyer, Jr. and T. K. Srull (eds.), *Handbook of Social Cognition*. Hillsdale, NJ: Erlbaum, 2nd edn 1994, 1–40.
18 W. James, *The Principles of Psychology*, vols. I & II, 1890.
19 Maréchal, 'An evolutionary perspective on the economics of energy consumption', 81.
20 G. Foyster (13 May 2011), 'The green brain', *G Magazine*, online, www.gmagazine.com.au/features/2553/green-brain (accessed June 2011).
21 Maréchal, 'An evolutionary perspective on the economics of energy consumption', 81.
22 PsyBlog (21 September 2009), *How Long to Form a Habit?*, PsyBlog, online, www.spring.org.uk/2009/09/how-long-to-form-a-habit.php (accessed June 2011).
23 P. Lally, C. H. M. van Jaarsveld, H. W. W. Potts, and J. Wardle, 'How are habits formed: modelling habit formation in the real world', *European Journal of Social Psychology*, 40, 2010, 998–1009.

18 Don't ask (tell)

1 Noah J. Goldstein, Robert B. Cialdini, and Vladas Griskevicius, 'A room with a viewpoint: using social norms to motivate environmental conservation in hotels', *Journal of Consumer Research: An Interdisciplinary Quarterly* (Chicago), 35(3), 2008, 472–82.
2 *Ibid.* 472.
3 The company that supplies towel reuse cards to hotels claims 75% of guests participate in towel reuse. Goldstein *et al.* observe a lower compliance in their experiment partly or wholly explained by the fact that they only test for compliance on guests' first eligible day irrespective of their length of stay whereas the 75% claim from the towel reuse card suppliers relates to a single act of compliance at any point in guests' stay, and lower compliance is partly or wholly explained by the fact that Goldstein *et al.* used strict criteria to record towel reuse compliance by guests and in so doing discounted towels hung on doorknobs or door hooks in order to eliminate unintentional compliance despite this being a common practice for towel recyclers.
4 C. R. Sunstein, 'Social norms and social rules', Environmental Law, John M. Olin Law & Economics Working Paper No. 36 (2nd series), 1995, 13.
5 Goldstein *et al.*, 'A room with a viewpoint', 480.
6 R. B. Cialdini, L. J. Demaine, B. J. Sagarin, D. W. Barrett, K. Rhoads, and P. L. Winter, 'Managing social norms for persuasive impact', *Social Influence*, 1(1), 2006, 3-15.
7 *Ibid.* 5.
8 *Ibid.* 11.
9 *Ibid.* 6.
10 *Ibid.* 12.

11 S. J. Dubner (13 October 2009), *Who Will Climb the Piano Stairs?*, Freakonomics Blog, online, www.freakonomics.com/2009/10/13/who-will-climb-the-piano-stairs/?replytocom=82127 (accessed July 2011).
12 M. Wenzel, 'Misperceptions of social norms about tax compliance (2): a field experiment', Research School of Social Sciences, Australian National University, Working Paper No. 8, June 2001, 1-26.
13 *Ibid.* 21.
14 C. R. Sunstein, 'Endogenous preferences, environmental law', John M. Olin Law & Economics Working Paper No. 14 (2nd series), 23.
15 A. Corner *et al.*, 'Communicating climate change to mass public audiences', Climate Change Communication Advisory Group (CCCAG), Working Document September 2010, pp. 1-15.
16 Sunstein, 'Endogenous preferences, environmental law', 33.

19 Make the question irrelevant

1 I. Ayres and B. Nalebuff (4 September 2006), *Easy Savings*, Forbes.com, online, www.forbes.com/forbes/2006/0904/146.html (accessed July 2011).
2 D. Lockton (5 January 2009), *Staggering Insight*, Design With Intent Blog, online, http://architectures.danlockton.co.uk/2009/01/05/staggering-insight/ (accessed July 2011).
3 United States Diplomatic Mission to Germany, *Poor Richard, 173,* The Library of America, online, http://usa.usembassy.de/etexts/funddocs/loa/bf1735.htm (accessed July 2011).
4 De Proverbio (1995) *Volume 1, Number 1,* Electronic Journal of International Proverb Studies, University of Tasmania, Australia, online, www.deproverbio.com/DPjournal/DP,1,1,95/FRANKLIN.html#Note15 (accessed July 2011).
5 G. V. Hudson, 'On seasonal time-adjustment in countries south of lat. 30°', *Transactions and Proceedings of the New Zealand Institute*, 28, 1895, 734.
6 Parliamentary Debates, House of Commons, 12 February 1908, columns 155–6. http://hansard.millbanksystems.com/commons/1908/feb/12/daylight-saving-bill#S4V0184P0_19080212_HOC_254.
7 D. Prerau, *Saving the Daylight: Why We Put the Clocks Forward*, London: Granta Books, 2006, 1–224.
8 B. Wansink, J. E. Painter, and J. North, 'Bottomless bowls: why visual cues of portion size may influence intake', *Obesity Research*, 13, 2005, 93–100. www.nature.com/oby/journal/v13/n1/full/oby200512a.html.

Glossary

1 S. Silberman (24 August 2009), *Placebos Are Getting More Effective. Drugmakers Are Desperate to Know Why*, *Wired* magazine, online, www.wired.com/medtech/drugs/magazine/17-09/ff_placebo_effect?currentPage=all (accessed Jan 2012).

Index